How to Pass

HIGHER

Modern Studies

Frank Cooney, Steph O'Reilly and Mary Clare McGinty

HODDER
GIBSON
AN HACHETTE UK COMPANY

The Publishers would like to thank the following for permission to reproduce copyright material:

Photo credits page 7 top © Marco Saracco – Fotolia.com; page 7 bottom © roger Pilkington – Fotolia.com; page 11 top © REX; page 11 bottom © REX/Duncan Bryceland; page 20 © ANDY BUCHANAN / Stringer / Getty Images; page 25 © REX/Ken McKay/ITV; page 37 © REX/Robert Perry; page 39 © Douglas Carr / Alamy; page 49 © britstock images ltd / Alamy; page 57 top © Scottish Children's Reporter Administration; page 57 bottom © Children's Hearings Scotland; page 61 © Dominic Cocozza ; page 70 © User:Wapcaplet / Wikimedia Commons (http://creativecommons.org/licenses/by-sa/3.0/deed.en); page 76 left © Denis Tangney Jr / Getty Images; page 76 right © Edward Parker / Alamy; page 80 top Courtesy of PhiLiP via Wikimedia Commons, Translation by Peter17 (http://creativecommons.org/licenses/by-sa/3.0/deed.en); page 80 bottom © REX/ZUMA; page 87 © djama – Fotolia.com; page 88 © David South / Alamy; page 92 © STR / Stringer / Getty Images; page 95 top © kosmozoo / Getty Images; page 95 bottom left © African National Congress; page 95 bottom right © National Freedom Party; page 96 top left © Democratic Alliance; page 96 top right © United Democratic Movement; page 96 centre left © Economic Freedom Fighters; page 96 centre right © Congress of the People; page 96 bottom © Inkatha Freedom Party; page 107 © Laurent VAN DER STOCKT / Getty Images; page 113 © Oxfam

Acknowledgements Exam question copyright © Scottish Qualifications Authority (p 32; the model answer does not emanate from SQA); An extract from p14 of 'Equally Well: Report of the Ministerial Task Force on Health Inequalities' produced by The Scottish Government 2008 (http://www.scotland.gov.uk/Resource/Doc/229649/0062206.pdf) © Crown copyright 2008. Contains public sector information licensed under the Open Government Licence v3.0. (p 48); Exam question copyright © Scottish Qualifications Authority (p 52; the model answer does not emanate from SQA); Extracts taken from http://www.scra.gov.uk/publications/online_statistical_service.cfm © Scottish Children's Reporter Administration and http://www.scra.gov.uk/children_s_hearings_system/index.cfm © Children's Hearings Scotland (pp 56–58); An extract adapted from the article 'More than 5000 join anti-rape midnight protest' by Martin Williams, from The Herald, 10 June 2014 © Herald & Times Group (p 61); Extracts from www.gov.uk and www.sps.gov.uk © Crown Copyright. Contains public sector information licensed under the Open Government Licence v3.0. (pp 64–65); An extract from The Fall of the ANC by Prince Mashele and Mzukisi Qobo, published by Picador Africa 2014, an imprint of Pan Macmillan (p 94); Exam question copyright © Scottish Qualifications Authority (pp 120–21; the model answer does not emanate from SQA); Charts adapted from 'National Voting Intention: the impact of the first debate – How would you vote if there were a General Election tomorrow' taken from General Election 2010, The Leaders' Debates, The worms' final verdict – lessons to be learned 30 April 2010, by Ipsos Mori. Chart A 'Before the first debate: 21–23 March' (Base: All certain to vote = 833 unweighted; data collected among 1503 British adults 18+, 19th–22nd March 2010). Chart B: 'After the first debate: 18th–19th April (Base: All certain to vote = 802 unweighted; data collected among 1253 British adults 18+, 18th–19th April 2010). Reproduced by kind permission of Ipsos MORI (p 121); Exam question copyright © Scottish Qualifications Authority (pp 122–24; the model answer does not emanate from SQA).

Every effort has been made to trace all copyright holders, but if any have been inadvertently overlooked the Publishers will be pleased to make the necessary arrangements at the first opportunity.

Although every effort has been made to ensure that website addresses are correct at time of going to press, Hodder Gibson cannot be held responsible for the content of any website mentioned in this book. It is sometimes possible to find a relocated web page by typing in the address of the home page for a website in the URL window of your browser.

Hachette UK's policy is to use papers that are natural, renewable and recyclable products and made from wood grown in sustainable forests. The logging and manufacturing processes are expected to conform to the environmental regulations of the country of origin.

Orders: please contact Bookpoint Ltd, 130 Milton Park, Abingdon, Oxon OX14 4SB. Telephone: (44) 01235 827720. Fax: (44) 01235 400454. Lines are open 9.00–5.00, Monday to Saturday, with a 24-hour message answering service. Visit our website at www.hoddereducation.co.uk. Hodder Gibson can be contacted direct on: Telephone: 0141 848 1609; Fax: 0141 889 6315; email: hoddergibson@hodder.co.uk.

© Frank Cooney, Steph O'Reilly, Mary Clare McGinty 2015

First published in 2015 by
Hodder Gibson, an imprint of Hodder Education,
An Hachette UK Company
2a Christie Street
Paisley PA1 1NB

Impression number   5 4 3 2

Year   2020 2019 2018 2017 2016

Cover photo © Yadvigagr/Dreamstime.com – Globe With 28 European Union Countries And Flags Photo
Illustrations by Aptara, Inc.
Typeset in 13/15 Cronos Pro Light by Aptara, Inc.
Printed in India.
A catalogue record for this title is available from the British Library.
ISBN: 978 1 4718 3597 1

Contents

Introduction

This revision book will help you to achieve the best possible result in your CfE Higher Modern Studies examination by explaining clearly what you need to know about the exam and what knowledge and skills you will need to display.

Access to the Hodder Gibson *CfE Higher Modern Studies* textbooks will enhance the use of this revision guide. Each of these books (and this *How to Pass*) has been endorsed by the Scottish Qualifications Authority.

The textbooks are:
● Democracy in Scotland and the UK
● Social Issues in the UK
● International Issues.

You have already covered all or most of the skills and knowledge required to pass the exam but revision has a very important role to play. By working your way through this book you will find it much easier to understand what you need to display in your assessment answers. This will enhance your confidence and enable you to achieve your full potential.

You will also find advice about the assignment, in which you will apply research and decision-making skills in the context of a Modern Studies topic or issue of your own choice. This assignment is important as it will be marked by SQA and will contribute to your overall mark and grade.

We hope you will find this book of great value and support.

Good luck!

Part One: How you will be tested

The CfE Higher award is made up of internally and externally marked assessments. To achieve the award, you need to pass the internal assessment for each of the following units:

- Democracy in Scotland and the United Kingdom
- Social Issues in the United Kingdom
- International Issues.

You also need to pass the Added Value unit for CfE Higher. This is an externally marked assessment that consists of two parts:

- Higher question paper (60 marks)
- Higher assignment (30 marks).

Total marks available: 90 marks

The marks you achieve in the question paper and assignment are added together and an overall mark will indicate a pass or fail. From this, your course award will then be graded.

Chapter 1
The exam

The question paper

The question paper is worth a total of 60 marks, with up to 20 marks awarded for each of the three units. Essay questions will be allocated 44 marks in total. The duration of the exam is two hours and 15 minutes.

What types of questions will I need to answer?

There are two types of skills questions that you will have practised in class. These are:

1 Using sources of information to identify **to what extent it is accurate to state that ...**
2 Using sources of information to identify **what conclusions can be drawn**.

In Part Five of this book we will look at examples of skills-based questions and students' answers.

In the knowledge section of your exam you will answer four types of questions:

- **Discuss: 20-mark extended response**, for example:
  A world power has influence and power in international relations. Discuss with reference to a world power you have studied.
- **To what extent: 20-mark extended response**, for example:
  To what extent has a world issue you have studied been resolved by international organisations?
- **Evaluate: 12-mark extended response**, for example:
  One aim of an electoral system is to provide fair representation. Evaluate the effectiveness of an electoral system you have studied in providing fair representation.
  You should refer to the electoral system used in Scotland or the United Kingdom or both in your answer.
- **Analyse: 12-mark extended response**, for example:
  Analyse the different lifestyle choices that may result in poor health.

Do I have choice?

Your teacher will usually have chosen one topic from each of the three units for you to study and you will answer questions on these topics in your exam. In Democracy in Scotland and the UK there will be a mandatory (compulsory) section covering Scotland's place in the UK political system and usually you will then concentrate on either the UK or the Scottish dimension. Your teacher will choose from the options listed opposite for each unit.

Remember

In your exam, the skills-based questions can appear in any two of the three units.

Remember

In your course exam, the knowledge and skills questions for International Issues will not refer to a particular country or a particular issue. You will be expected to base your answer on your knowledge and understanding of your studied world power or issue.

Unit of the course	Option one	Option two
Democracy in Scotland and the UK	Democracy in Scotland	Democracy in the UK
Social Issues in the UK	Social Inequality	Crime and the Law
International Issues	World Powers	World Issues

Hints & tips ★

What makes a good knowledge answer?

- One that answers the question and only provides knowledge and understanding and analysis/evaluation that is **relevant** to the question.
- One that is an **appropriate length**. Use the number of marks assigned to each question as a guide to how much you should write and how much time to devote to the question. An answer to a 20-mark extended writing question should include greater higher-order skills of analysis and evaluation and a more structured answer than one to a 12-mark question.
- One that uses **up-to-date** examples to illustrate your understanding of the question being asked.
- One that includes a **range** of points, detailed explanation and description and accurate exemplification, analysis and evaluation.

What makes a bad knowledge answer?

- One that does not answer the question, or tries to change the question being asked. This is sometimes called 'turning a question'.
- One that gives detailed description or explanation that is not relevant to the question.
- One that contains information that is out of date (you should be especially careful of this in the International Issues unit).
- One that simply consists of a list of facts with no development. You must tailor your answer to the question, and only give information that is relevant to what is being asked.

Chapter 2
The assignment

Before your exam in May, you will carry out the assignment as part of your CfE Higher course assessment. Your teacher will probably plan to complete this during the spring term before you sit the exam.

What is the assignment?

The assignment will apply research and decision-making skills in the context of a Modern Studies issue. You can choose a political, social or international issue. The information collected should display knowledge and understanding of the topic or issue chosen. SQA recommend that you should devote about eight hours for the research stage, including preparation time for the production of evidence.

The results of the research will be written up under controlled assessment conditions and must be completed within one hour and 30 minutes. The assignment is very important as it is worth a total of 30 marks.

You are allowed to bring two single-sided sheets of A4 paper (containing your research evidence) into the exam to refer to during the write-up. This is referred to as 'research evidence' and consists of materials collected during the research stage of the assignment.

What type of issue should I choose?

With agreement from your teacher, you should choose a topic or issue that enables you to make a decision about an issue, for example: 'The voting age in all Scottish and UK elections should be reduced to sixteen.'

Some possible other titles could include:
- The House of Lords should be replaced by an elected second chamber.
- Free prescriptions should be available to all UK citizens.
- Russia should be allowed to retain Crimea.
- The US Electoral College should be abolished.
- The winter fuel allowance for elderly people should be means tested.
- All Scottish police officers should be issued with Taser guns.

Where do I gather information from?

The information gathered for your research can be broken down into two parts: *primary information* and *secondary information*.

Primary information

Primary information is evidence that you have gathered by yourself and is unique to your personal research. The ways in which you gather primary evidence can vary greatly – some examples are given below:
- surveys/questionnaires
- interviews
- emails

- letters
- focus groups
- field study.

Secondary information

Secondary information is evidence that you have gathered from research that was carried out by others. You should use it to help support your personal research. There are vast amounts of secondary information available, in many different formats – just a few examples are below:

- school textbooks, newspapers and magazines
- internet search engines and websites
- TV and radio programmes
- mobile phone apps
- social media such as Twitter
- library books and articles.

How do I plan my research?

To carry out a successful piece of personal research, you need to plan it effectively. You will need to keep all evidence of your planning so that your work can be accurately marked.

You may wish to consider the following questions about your primary and secondary sources:

- What useful information have I gained from this source to help me research my issue?
- How reliable is the information gathered from the source?
- Could the source contain bias or exaggeration?

How is the assignment marked?

The allocation of marks is based on the following criteria:

1 Identifying and displaying knowledge and understanding of the issue about which a decision is to be made, including alternative courses of action – up to a maximum of **10 marks**
   You should agree an issue to research with your teacher. It has to relate to one or more of the issues that you study in your course:
   - Democracy in Scotland and the United Kingdom
   - Social Issues in the United Kingdom
   - International Issues.

2 Synthesising and analysing information from a range of sources, including use of specified resources – up to a maximum of **10 marks**. You will research a wide range of sources to provide contrasting views on your chosen issue. By linking information from a variety of sources and viewpoints, you will be able to enrich and synthesise the arguments that are developed in your report.

Remember

Five of the 10 marks are available for referencing the sources in your research evidence A4 sheets. Without direct referencing, a maximum of 5 is all that can be achieved.

3 Evaluating the usefulness and reliability of a range of sources of information – up to a maximum of **2 marks**. To achieve 2 marks, a comparative judgement of the sources must be made.

   You will comment on the background and nature of the source. Does it provide only one point of view? Are its findings up to date, and so are its comments still relevant today?

4 Communicating information using the convention of a report – up to a maximum of **4 marks**.

   Remember that you are not writing an essay; you are considering the arguments for and against a proposal. You should write in the form of a report and include subheadings.

   Here you should make conclusions relevant to the research issue.

   Try to avoid repeating findings you have already given.

5 Reaching a decision, supported by evidence, about the issue – up to a maximum of **4 marks**.

   The decision should be based on the body of evidence you have provided in the report.

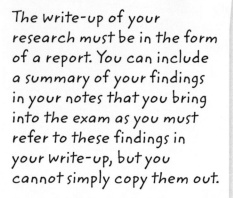

Remember

The write-up of your research must be in the form of a report. You can include a summary of your findings in your notes that you bring into the exam as you must refer to these findings in your write-up, but you cannot simply copy them out.

Remember

You should choose an issue with alternative viewpoints. For guidance, you could look at the old Higher Paper 2 Decision-making exam papers.

Part Two: Democracy in Scotland and the UK

The UK and Scottish parliament buildings

Chapter 3
UK constitutional arrangements and voting system

UK constitutional arrangements

The UK is a parliamentary democracy with a constitutional monarch who has effectively no political power. The **royal prerogatives** held by the monarch, such as the power to dissolve parliament, are in actual fact held by the prime minister, who is in turn responsible to an elected House of Commons. The Queen is the head of state to the people of England, Scotland, Northern Ireland and Wales and to the peoples of the fifteen realms of the Commonwealth. Figure 3.1 below illustrates the political system of the UK. Parliamentary sovereignty ensures all powers are vested in the UK parliament and the powers granted to the **devolved** governments can be returned to the UK parliament and the devolved parliaments abolished.

However, membership of the European Union and acceptance of the European Convention on Human Rights (ECHR) places limits on parliamentary sovereignty (see pages 10–11).

> ## Key words
>
> **Royal prerogatives:** Powers of the monarch that are exercised in the crown's name by the prime minister and government ministers.
>
> **Devolved:** Powers that have been transferred from central government to local or regional administration.

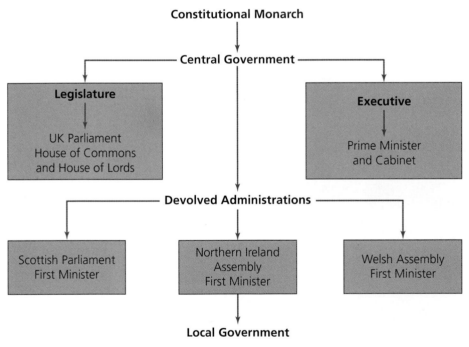

Figure 3.1 The structure of the UK political system

The UK central government has responsibility for national affairs, such as the economy, defence, foreign policy and the environment. In the UK, the prime minister leads the government with the support of the cabinet and ministers. Departments and their agencies are responsible for putting government policy into practice.

The role and powers of the devolved bodies

In Northern Ireland, Scotland and Wales, some government policies and public services are different from those in England. The UK central government has given certain powers to devolved governments, so that they can make decisions for their own areas. The Scottish Parliament, the National Assembly for Wales and the Northern Ireland Assembly were established and took control in 1999. The arrangements are different for each, reflecting their history and administrative structures. The UK government remains responsible for national policy on all matters that have not been devolved, including foreign affairs, defence, social security and trade (see Table 3.1). The implementation of the Smith Commission proposals will lead to changes in the powers listed in Table 3.1.

Reserved issues	Devolved powers
Constitutional matters	Education and training
UK foreign policy	Health
UK defence and national security	Local government
Fiscal, economic and monetary system	Social work
Immigration and nationality	Housing
Energy: electricity, coal, gas and nuclear energy	Planning
Common markets	Tourism, economic development and financial assistance to industry
Trade and industry, including competition and customer protection	Some aspects of transport, including the Scottish road network, bus policy and ports and harbours
Some aspects of transport, including railways, transport safety and regulation	Law and home affairs, including most aspects of criminal and civil law, the prosecution system and the courts
Employment legislation	Police and fire services
Social security	The environment
Gambling and the National Lottery	Natural and built heritage
Data protection	Agriculture, forestry and fishing
Abortion, human fertilisation, embryology and genetics	Sport and the arts
Equal opportunities	

Table 3.1 Reserved issues and devolved powers

Scottish Parliament

The Scottish Parliament debates topical issues and passes laws on devolved matters that affect Scotland. It also scrutinises the work and policies of the Scottish Government. It is made up of 129 elected Members of the Scottish Parliament (MSPs) and meets at Holyrood in Edinburgh. Since 1999, the Scottish Parliament has held responsibility for the powers devolved to Scotland. These devolved powers, such as education, are listed in Table 3.1. However, more powers continue to be devolved to Scotland. As part of the 2012 Scotland Act, MSPs at Holyrood will be responsible for some tax powers, air guns and drink-driving limits (which came into force in December 2014). However, the SNP and members of the general public believe that Holyrood should hold even further powers, often referred to as 'devo-max'. On 18 September 2014 the Scottish electorate voted to remain part of the UK by 55 per cent to 45 per cent.

Welsh Assembly

The National Assembly for Wales is the representative body that holds law-making powers on devolved matters. It debates and approves legislation. The role of the Assembly is to scrutinise and monitor the Welsh Assembly Government. It has 60 elected members and meets in the Senedd.

Northern Ireland Assembly

The Northern Ireland Assembly was established as part of the Belfast Agreement (also known as the Good Friday Agreement) in 1998. Devolution to Northern Ireland was suspended in October 2002 and restored on 8 May 2007.

The impact of EU membership on decision-making in the UK

The UK has been a member of the EU since 1973 and this membership has had a significant impact on the UK's political system. Arguably the greatest impact on decision-making is that EU law takes precedence over UK law. This means that laws passed by parliament that conflict with EU law are illegal. This situation clearly contradicts the main principle of the UK constitution that parliament is **sovereign**. This also means that UK judges have a higher court – the European Court of Justice – to which they can refer suspected infringements of EU law. A further implication of EU membership on decision-making in the UK is that the prime minister is regularly involved in European Council or Summit meetings with other EU leaders. Also, members of the Cabinet take part in monthly Council of Ministers meetings. At every Council meeting, each country sends the minister for the policy field to be discussed, for example the environment minister will attend the meeting dealing with environmental matters, known as the Environment Council.

Critics argue that because the prime minister or Cabinet ministers make EU law in these meetings, this weakens the scrutiny function of parliament as it only has the power to approve or reject EU legislation that comes into force in the UK.

The UK government retains sovereignty over most areas of public expenditure, such as social security, health, housing and transport; however, in areas of single-market regulation (the free movement of

> **Key word**
>
> **Sovereign:** Possessing supreme power.

goods, capital, services and people) the UK's decision-making powers are constrained by EU membership.

EU membership is one of the main reserved powers of Westminster. This means that the Scottish Parliament and the Welsh and Northern Irish Assemblies have had a limited engagement with the EU. The main impact is that these assemblies are now responsible for implementing EU law where the power has been devolved to them.

Under pressure from UKIP, David Cameron has promised to hold a **referendum** on British membership of the EU if he is still in power after the 2015 General Election.

Key word

Referendum: The electorate, not their representatives, vote to accept or reject a proposal.

Independence Referendum

Issues and debates around recent and proposed changes to the role and powers of the Scottish and UK Parliaments

On 18 September 2014 the people of Scotland were asked the question 'Should Scotland be an independent country?' in the Independence Referendum.

In the weeks and months leading up to the referendum, the 'Better Together' and 'Yes Scotland' campaigns debated the issue fervently. Debates over the issue of independence took place on television, in communities and within universities and societies.

Better Together

The Better Together campaign was the pro-union and anti-independence campaign. It was officially launched on 25 June 2012 and was fronted by the former UK Chancellor Alistair Darling and supported by Labour, the Conservatives and the Liberal Democrats. Its principal aim was to convince people living in Scotland to vote 'no' on 18 September 2014. In June 2014 Better Together adopted the slogan 'No thanks' in a bid to sound more positive about the UK remaining together; it also adopted the slogan 'We get the best of both worlds as part of the United Kingdom.'

Figure 3.2 The Better Together campaign

Yes Scotland

The Yes Scotland campaign was headed by Alex Salmond and was officially launched on 25 May 2012. It was an alliance between the Scottish National Party, the Scottish Green Party and the Scottish Socialist Party. The campaign aimed to persuade those voting in the referendum that voting for an independent Scotland was the best decision.

Figure 3.2 The Yes Scotland campaign

For	Against
National debt	
Alex Salmond stressed that Scotland would have been committed to honouring its share of the UK national debt but only if given a share of the assets, including the pound.	Alistair Darling maintained that a currency union would not be possible in the event of independence and Scotland could not demand 'the best of both worlds'.
The NHS	
Sir Harry Burns, former Chief Medical Officer for Scotland, announced the week before the referendum that an independent Scotland was necessary to secure the future of the NHS, as NHS cuts, charging and privatisation become an ever-increasing aspect of the NHS.	Better Together argued that as health is a devolved issue, Scotland will always be able to protect the NHS from privatisation. They argued that the Nationalists were scaremongering to win votes.
Oil	
Alex Salmond argued that about £1 billion – one-tenth of the oil revenues – could have formed an oil fund similar to the one operated in Norway. Yes Scotland was convinced that Scottish oil estimates were accurate and that the revenue created would contribute to Scotland's success as an independent country.	Opponents of Scottish independence argued that Yes Scotland overestimated the wealth that could be created by North Sea oil. Sir Ian Wood, the oil billionaire, warned that the Yes Scotland campaign was wrong to say that 24 billion barrels are left and the figure is more likely to be 15–16 billion barrels.
Currency	
The Scottish Government argued that it would be in the best interests of both an independent Scotland and the rest of the UK for Scotland to share the pound and retain the Bank of England as a lender of last resorts to bail out Scottish-based banks if needed. They pointed to the case of Belgium and Luxembourg, who have successfully been in a currency union for decades.	The UK **Coalition Government**, along with the Labour Party, ruled out the possibility of a currency union with Scotland. Instead, they suggested that Scotland could either use the pound in the same way that Panama uses the US dollar, set up a new currency or use the euro.
The European Union	
Nationalists argued that Scotland would not have to reapply to join the EU as citizens would continue to be EU citizens after a period of negotiation of Scotland's new terms.	Unionists argued that if Scotland had voted to leave the UK, it would have voted to leave an EU member state and would therefore have to reapply as a new member state, relying on the support of governments such as Spain, which would not support such an application.
Nuclear weapons/defence	
Yes Scotland argued that an independent Scotland would be free from nuclear weapons, which are currently stored on the Clyde. They also argued that Scotland would join NATO but focus a new Scottish army's effort on humanitarian work.	It was argued that storage of nuclear weapons on the Clyde provided jobs for people in the local community and that in the event of a Yes vote it would be extremely expensive for these to be relocated. Better Together also argued that a nuclear-free Scotland would not be granted NATO membership.

Table 3.2 Key points for and against independence

> ## Key word
> **Coalition Government:** When two or more political parties form a government.

Result of the 2014 Scottish Independence Referendum

On 18 September 2014, the Scottish electorate was asked 'Should Scotland be an independent country?' After two years of bitter campaigning by both sides, 85 per cent of Scottish people turned out to vote in the referendum. In some regions, such as East Dunbartonshire and Stirling, turnout was over 90 per cent, the highest turnout ever recorded in a UK election or referendum. Forty-five per cent of the electorate voted for Scotland to become an independent country, with 55 per cent voting to remain part of the UK. Many local authorities were won and lost within a very narrow margin. Four councils saw a majority vote 'Yes': Dundee, Glasgow, North Lanarkshire and West Dunbartonshire. This resulted in claims from many that the poorest in society had voted for change while in more affluent areas people were more likely to vote to remain part of the UK. However, it was widely acknowledged that even a 'No' vote was not a vote for the *status quo* and that the people of Scotland all demanded change.

Alex Salmond announced that he would stand down as party leader and as First Minister. Nicola Sturgeon was elected party leader and became the first woman First Minister, making all three leaders of the main political parties in Scotland women. However, Labour leader Johann Lamont resigned in October 2014. Jim Murphy, a Labour MP, was elected as the new Scottish Labour leader in December 2014.

Implications of the 2014 Scottish Independence Referendum

One of the most positive outcomes of the referendum was that the people of Scotland had become better engaged with politics. As Alex Salmond stated after the result was declared: 'Scotland now has the most politically engaged population in western Europe and one of the most engaged in any country, anywhere in the democratic world.' This will likely have great implications for Scottish politics in the future.

In spite of the result, the referendum guaranteed major changes to the UK's constitutional structure, with immediate calls for an English parliament from some sections of society and a general consensus on the need for more regional powers to be granted across the UK. The primary implication for Scotland is the new powers that were guaranteed from all members of Better Together. Lord Smith of Kelvin assumed responsibility for overseeing a new Scottish Devolution Commission to implement the cross-party decision to give more powers to Scotland.

However, the referendum result also affects people living in other parts of the union. The day after the result was declared, David Cameron announced that he would use the outcome to implement longstanding Conservative plans to reform Commons rules to stop English MPs being overruled on English-only matters by the votes of Scottish MPs, settling the **West Lothian question**. All three main UK parties are broadly in agreement on further powers for Scotland, but the 'English votes for English laws' plan is likely to prove highly controversial because of the danger of parliament having two classes of MP.

Key word

West Lothian question: The question was asked by Tam Dalyell in 1977. It asks why Scottish MPs have the same right to vote at Westminster as any English MP now that large areas of policy are devolved to the Scottish parliament in areas such as health, housing, schools and policing.

Electoral systems and voting behaviour

UK general elections are held every five years. In UK elections, the electoral system used is known as First Past The Post (FPTP). In 2011, a referendum was held on replacing FPTP with the Alternative Vote (AV) – a modified version of FPTP. However, on a low turnout voters rejected AV. In Scotland elections take place every four years. In Scottish parliamentary elections and local council elections Proportional Representation (PR) is used. For Scottish Parliament elections the PR system used is called the Additional Member System (AMS). For Scottish local council elections the Single Transferable Vote (STV) is used. Party List (PL) is the type of PR used in European elections.

First Past The Post

First Past The Post (FPTP) is the electoral system used in UK general elections. It is a simple majority system whereby in each of the UK's 650 constituencies the candidate with the most votes wins the seat and becomes the MP in that constituency.

Arguments for FPTP	Arguments against FPTP
FPTP is easy to understand – a particular benefit for elderly and first-time voters.	FPTP does not produce a proportional result. This means that the percentage of votes received using FPTP does not compare with the percentage of seats gained. This is unfair and means that winners are over-represented. In 2010, the Conservatives gained 47.2 per cent of the seats in Westminster with only 36.1 per cent of the votes.
The voter simply has to mark an X next to the candidate of their choice on the ballot paper and the candidate who receives the most votes in that constituency wins the seat in parliament. The result of this simple and easy-to-understand system is that it will often encourage voter turnout. In 2010, 66 per cent of people turned out to vote in the general election, compared to 56 per cent of voters for the more complicated Scottish elections.	It can result in a lot of wasted votes. As it is the person with the most votes who wins the constituency, all the other votes are discounted and individuals do not have their votes heard. This can result in **voter apathy** as voters feel that their votes do not count.
The results of the elections are produced very quickly. The votes are counted for each of the candidates in a constituency and whoever gets the most wins. This is a reasonably quick process and consequently the result of the election is announced the next day. In 2010 in Houghton, Sunderland, the winning candidate was announced only 52 minutes after the polling stations were closed.	FPTP is unfair to smaller parties. Smaller parties that only get a low percentage of votes will gain no representation because they do not win in any constituency. In 2005, despite achieving 250,000 votes, the Green Party won no seats in Westminster. The DUP actually won fewer votes but won nine seats in Parliament. (In 2010, the Green Party had only one MP in the House of Commons despite gaining 265,187 votes.)
FPTP usually produces a clear winner and avoids minority governments or coalitions. The 2010 General Election did, however, produce a coalition government between the Conservatives and the Liberal Democrats, although this is a rare example and the first time that the winning party did not have an overall majority since 1974.	FPTP favours larger parties. The bigger parties are more likely to win in constituencies and gain more MPs. As the number of votes across all constituencies is not added up, this favours the larger parties. Since 1945, with the exception of 2010, all governments in the UK have either been Labour or Conservative.
FPTP retains a strong MP–constituency link. The electorate votes directly for an MP and once the MP is elected the constituents are fully aware of who they are and can hold them accountable for their actions. In contrast, under Proportional Representation systems, more than one representative can be elected.	The winning MP may not have a majority of the votes cast; in 1992 a Liberal Democrat candidate won with only 26 per cent of the vote.

Table 3.3 Arguments for and against FPTP

Additional Member System

The Scottish Parliament, Welsh Assembly and London Assembly are all elected using the Additional Member System (AMS). This system is a mixture of First Past The Post and Proportional Representation (PR). In Scotland, voters cast two votes. The first vote is used to elect the 73 constituency MSPs. The second vote uses the Party List system of PR. In this vote, the electorate choose between parties who will represent them in their region. There are eight regions and each region elects seven MSPs, making the total number of MSPs 129.

Key word

Voter apathy: A lack of interest or engagement in the political process.

Arguments for AMS	Arguments against AMS
As there are two ballot papers, AMS is more proportional. One uses FPTP and the other uses the Party/Regional List. In 2011, the SNP won 45.4 per cent of the vote in the Scottish Parliament election and this translated into 69 seats, or 53.4 per cent of the seats available – a far more proportional outcome than FPTP would allow.	AMS is more complicated for voters to understand as it features two votes, and this can confuse some voters who are used to voting using FPTP in British elections. In the 2007 Scottish Parliament elections, a staggering 140,000 ballot papers were rejected.
AMS usually creates coalition governments. This is seen as an advantage because one party cannot force opinions upon the people, especially when they do not have more than 50 per cent of the vote. This is an advantage of AMS because coalitions can create consensus and agreement on policies. The 1999 and 2003 Scottish elections created coalition governments that passed many important laws in Scotland, such as the smoking ban. However, in 2011 a coalition government was not formed as the SNP won the Scottish Parliament's first majority government.	AMS often creates coalition governments. Although this is sometimes regarded as a strength of the system, it can also be deemed a weakness. The electorate never votes for a coalition government on their ballot paper. This means that they are not democratic. No one voted for the coalition between Labour and Liberal Democrats in Scotland from 1999 to 2007. Again, the SNP minority government of 2007–11 failed to get through some of its key policies, such as minimum pricing of alcohol.
AMS allows for greater voter choice as there are two votes. In the first vote, one MSP is elected per constituency. In the second vote, cast using PR, seven MSPs are elected to each region. Voters in Glasgow Kelvin can vote for a constituency candidate like Sandra White of the SNP, but could vote for a totally different party, such as the Green Party, in the second regional vote. Therefore the electorate has more choice.	It can often be the case that smaller parties achieve too much power in AMS. AMS allows parties that have very little support to be involved in coalition governments, which can mean they have a say in decisions made and laws passed. The Liberal Democrats, whilst in the Scottish Government coalition, helped pass legislation such as free tuition fees and free care for the elderly despite only having around 15 per cent of the total vote.
AMS is fairer on smaller parties as it enables them to gain a percentage of seats equal to the percentage of votes they have gained by using PR in the second vote. The Green Party gained seats in the Scottish Parliament election despite never gaining any under FPTP.	The regional MSPs elected through the PR vote in AMS are not directly voted for by the people. The people vote for a party and the party decides which candidates will become MSPs. Also, very few people can hold them accountable for their actions as they do not know who they are.

Table 3.4 Arguments for and against AMS

Single Transferable Vote

The Single Transferable Vote (STV) was first used in Scottish local elections in May 2007. Voters rank the candidates in order of preference and can vote for as few or as many candidates as they like. A quota system is then used to calculate the minimum number of votes required to win a seat.

Arguments for STV	Arguments against STV
The STV system is more proportional as candidates must reach a certain 'quota' of votes to be elected, with all votes being counted and affecting the result. Therefore the percentage of votes is closer to the percentage of seats. In the 2007 Scottish Local Authority Elections, the SNP gained roughly the same percentage of seats within wards as they did votes, and big parties like Labour lost out.	STV is thought to be more confusing than many other electoral systems. The STV system means that people are asked to cast their vote more than once on the same ballot paper. This can confuse some voters who are used to voting using FPTP in British elections. Therefore it may discourage people from voting. In the 2007 Scottish Local Authority Elections, 100,000 people 'spoilt' their votes as they were confused about the voting system. These votes were not counted. Furthermore, voter turnout was only 32 per cent in some areas of Scotland.
STV is fairer to smaller parties and gives them a better chance of gaining seats. This means that STV allows small parties to gain a percentage of votes that matches the percentage of seats they have gained as it is a Proportional Representation system. Therefore smaller parties gain a larger percentage of support. In 2012, there were 22 councillors representing the smaller parties of Scotland, such as the Green Party.	STV can often produce results to which no one agreed. STV produces a result that means many local authorities have no party with overall control. Therefore it is hard to make decisions and often parties need to form coalitions at local level to be able to make decisions. No one actually voted for this and it is seen as undemocratic. In 2012, there were only 9 councils out of 32 that had a party with overall control, therefore coalitions or minority governments were formed. This can cause slow policy-making and indecision, such as in the case of the Edinburgh Tram system.
There are usually fewer wasted votes in STV. The voters must place candidates in order of preference; they can place as many or as few votes as they wish. As candidates must reach a certain 'quota' of votes then every vote cast must be counted. In 2012, the Liberal Democrats lost 95 seats in the local elections as people were able to cast votes for more than one party.	STV can allow more power to fall into the hands of smaller parties. STV allows parties that have very little support to be involved in coalition agreements, which can mean they have a say in decisions. Scottish Borders is an SNP/Independent/Liberal Democrat coalition. Therefore independent candidates have a lot of power.
STV allows more choice for the electorate. Voters can vote for as many or as few candidates as they wish. Therefore there is more choice about who they can vote for in terms of parties and candidates.	The results from STV take longer than other systems. The public is asked to vote for more than one candidate, and they can often cast up to as many as seven votes. Also the 'quota' can only be decided when the votes are all cast. Once this has happened the votes must be counted and then re-counted until a winner can be declared.

Table 3.5 Arguments for and against STV

National/regional Party List

This PL system was introduced for elections to the European Parliament in 1999. Each party draws up a list of candidates ranked according to the party's preference, with the more important candidates ranked at the top of the list. Electors then vote for a party rather than a person. Representatives are elected from eleven large multi-member regions, each electing between three and ten MEPs. In the 2014 European Elections, Scotland elected six MEPs.

Summary of 2014 European Elections

The 2014 European Elections were dominated by anti-establishment parties. There was a trend across Europe against pro-federalist politicians and towards Eurosceptic parties, with the largest federalist Alliance (the

European People's Party) losing 6 per cent of the Parliament. Although Eurosceptic Alliances increased their representation, they are still in the minority with approximately 25 per cent of seats.

In the UK 2014 European Elections, the UK Independence Party (UKIP) won with 27.5 per cent of the popular vote, against Labour (25.4 per cent) and Conservative (23.9 per cent). It was the first time since 1906 that a party other than Labour or the Conservatives had won a national election. In Scotland, UKIP won one of the six Scottish European seats, with the Liberal Democrats losing their only seat.

Arguments for PL	Arguments against PL
As party lists are a form of PR they enjoy the benefit of being proportional and every vote has an equal value.	The MP–constituent link is weaker as there is no one representative.
PL is a simple system for voters to use. The party selects the candidates who will appear on their list and the electorate simply votes for a political party. If a party gains 30 per cent of the vote, the top 30 per cent of their candidates will be elected.	Voters have no choice over the candidate elected as they only vote for a party, with the party leaders choosing the candidate.
It can help to ensure fairer representation of groups that are normally under-represented in the political system. Parties can put female and ethnic minority candidates at the top of their lists, increasing the likelihood that they will be elected.	PL can lead to under-representation as party leaders may choose people similar to them to stand, rather than candidates from under-represented groups such as women and ethnic minorities.
PL traditionally creates coalition governments and this results in a broader range of parties being represented.	The creation of coalitions can also be seen as a weakness of the PL system.
	As in other forms of PR, the balance of power can lie with smaller parties, which can be undemocratic.

Table 3.6 Arguments for and against Party List (PL)

Voting behaviour

Main factors that affect voting behaviour

There are several factors that affect voting behaviour. Some are short-term factors such as the media, party image, leadership style and policy issues, while others are long-term factors such as age, social class, ethnicity, gender and religion.

Long-term factors

Social class

From 1945 to 1970, there was a clear link between a person's voting behaviour and their class. At this time, 65 per cent of working-class people voted for Labour, while 85 per cent of the middle class voted for the Conservatives. However, there were always working-class people who voted Conservative and middle-class Labour voters. Since 1970, as a result of **class de-alignment**, there has been a decline in the importance of class as the main determinant of voting behaviour. More recent elections have provided evidence that social class is no longer so important in shaping political attitudes. In 1974 Labour won 57 per cent of working-class votes, but by the 2010 General Election this had fallen to 40 per cent. The Conservative Party in 1974 won 56 per cent of the middle-class vote, but this had fallen to 39 per cent in 2010.

Age

A person's age is a factor that influences voting behaviour as it not only determines who a person votes for but also if they will vote at all. Young voters will traditionally vote Labour, while older voters vote Conservative. This may be partly due to the perception that the Conservative Party will favour more traditional values. Furthermore, in the 2005 UK General Election, voting was much higher in the elderly group (65 and over), where older voters were more likely to vote at all than 18- to 26-year-olds, at 75 per cent versus 37 per cent.

Gender

Gender also affects voting behaviour. Women have historically been far more likely to vote for the Conservatives and to make up the majority of Tory voters. However, there have been recent changes and, in particular, the 1997 Election was significant because New Labour overcame this gender gap through their female-friendly policies. As a result, there were more women candidates and 101 Labour women MPs were elected. As women become more middle class and better educated, they are more likely to move to the left.

Ethnicity

Ethnicity is also an important factor in determining a person's voting behaviour. Black and Asian voters are more likely to vote for Labour, but it is also possible that this can be attributed to their social class, as many people from ethnic minorities in Britain are from lower socio-economic groups. However, there are also many affluent black and Asian voters who do not identify with Labour.

Short-term factors

Media

The media has, in recent elections, been a very important factor in affecting voter behaviour. In the 2010 General Election, 9.4 million people watched the first live TV debate, and *The Sun* newspaper was read by 8 million people every day (and for many voters this was their only source of information on the Election). The media is an important factor to consider as it can often influence other long- and short-term factors, for instance, regarding age, younger voters may be more likely to vote SNP as a result of the party's policies and image, yet this could also be because of the SNP's effective use of new media, such as Twitter, which are more often used by young than older voters. It can only be assumed that as

Key word

Class de-alignment: When voters no longer align themselves with a particular political party on the basis of their social class.

Remember

A voter will, of course, hold more than one of these long-term factors. Age, for example, cuts across class, gender and ethnicity.

Hints & tips

See pages 23–25 for further information on the media.

further advancements in the media continue to be made it will become an even more important factor in shaping voter attitudes.

Party leadership and policies

Party leadership is a factor that has come to be a greater influence on voter behaviour in recent elections. In the run-up to the 2011 Scottish Election, Alex Salmond appeared on the television programme *Question Time* and came across as a strong leader; meanwhile, the then Labour leader Iain Gray was ambushed in Glasgow's Central Station by public-sector cuts protestors. Rather than engaging with or ignoring the protesters, Iain Gray left the station and headed into a local Subway shop to seek refuge. He appeared weak and was ridiculed by the media. The outcome of the Election was that the SNP became the country's first majority government and Labour experienced severe losses, including in the traditional Labour heartlands of Glasgow and the West.

Similarly, in the 2010 UK General Election, Gordon Brown was deemed to be a dull and boring leader while David Cameron was regarded as stronger and more inspiring. Arguably, this difference in leadership style had an impact on voting behaviour. However, this could also be the result of the way in which the leaders were portrayed in the media. Voters will not only consider *who* they are voting for, in the form of the party leaders, but they will also look at *what* they are voting for, through the party manifesto and stance on issues. Voters will be affected by the issues and policies for which a party stands. In the run-up to elections, voters will assess which policies are closest to their own values and align themselves with a party accordingly.

Remember

Although many factors affect voting behaviour, some factors are more influential than others. Social class has always been an important factor that affects voting behaviour, but more recently short-term influences seem to have overtaken social class as the most important factors.

Figure 3.3 In the 2014 Scottish referendum, 16- and 17-year-olds were allowed to vote

Chapter 4
Influencing the political process

The role and influence of pressure groups

Representative democracy does not formally permit people to make policy and directly influence the decision-making process. Instead, it allows the general public to vote for a representative, such as MPs, MSPs and councillors, who work on their behalf. However, political participation in the UK is not confined to elections, as participation continues through the activities of pressure groups. Pressure groups are groups of individuals who come together, through a common belief or passion, to put pressure on the government to introduce, abolish or change something. These groups are formed by like-minded people who feel passionate about an issue and have the aim of protecting or advancing their shared interest.

There are two main types of pressure groups: cause groups and interest groups.

Cause groups

Also sometimes known as 'promotional pressure groups', cause groups generally campaign to raise awareness of specific causes. Cause groups can campaign on behalf of other people who cannot campaign for themselves – Shelter would be an example of such a cause group – or they can attempt to influence public opinion, for example Greenpeace is an environmental group that puts pressure on the government to help create a greener world.

Interest groups

Also sometimes known as 'sectional pressure groups', interest groups work to promote a particular interest, often to advance the economic or professional status of their members, such as the British Medical Association.

To what extent do pressure groups impact on the political system?

The effectiveness of pressure groups and the extent to which they influence politics depend on the type of pressure group. Pressure groups can be either *insider* or *outsider* groups and the status of the group reflects their relationship with the government and affects the extent to which they can influence the political system.

Many pressure groups are experts in their field, such as the British Medical Association. They are known as insider pressure groups. These insider groups regularly gain direct access to policy-makers, such as civil servants or government ministers. Insider groups may even be consulted by government in the law-making process, and so they can have great power and influence on legislation. They are in a privileged position as a result of their expertise and specialist knowledge. Ultimately, insider pressure groups are able to influence government decision-making.

On the other hand, outsider groups, with no access to parliament, often mount campaigns to influence the public, government and media. They try to persuade public opinion to their point of view through activities such as demonstrations and petitions. While this type of pressure-group behaviour may earn media and public attention, it often does not result in any sort of influence on government decision-making. In fact, illegal pressure-group methods can greatly hinder the success of the pressure group in influencing the government.

However, outsider pressure groups may be successful in influencing the government, who may listen to them as a result of concerns that the group may influence large swathes of the electorate. Outsider pressure groups continually lobby government and some will use professional **lobbying** organisations, which offer contacts and knowledge of the political system. Some also try to seek pledges from candidates at elections. This strategy is used by both pro-life and pro-choice groups, for example. Other groups will take unconstitutional action, such as Fathers for Justice, who are renowned for their illegal methods of gaining media coverage.

> ### Key word
> **Lobbying:** When individuals or pressure groups try to influence government decisions.

Do pressure groups enhance or threaten democracy?

Remember

In the debate about the effectiveness of pressure groups, you should discuss both the strengths and the weaknesses of them.

Enhance democracy

Pressure groups greatly benefit the political system as they allow for greater participation in the political process. This is regarded as a good thing because participation in the formal political process is dwindling. In particular, election turnout is low, as is political party membership. Therefore pressure-group participation enhances democracy in the UK. The Gurkha Justice Campaign stood up for the rights of the Gurkhas who had fought for the UK during the twentieth century but who were denied the same benefits as their British and Commonwealth equivalents. After a campaign led by Joanna Lumley, the government announced that any Gurkha who had fought in the British Army for four years or more, before 1997, would be given the right to settle in Britain.

Threaten democracy

It can also be argued that pressure groups are a threat to democracy. Unlike political parties, pressure groups are self-appointed and the public cannot vote them out in elections. This is regarded by many to be undemocratic. Pressure groups are capable of forcing minority views as they are well organised and well structured. Some pressure groups carry out illegal methods to raise their profile and gain media attention. This happened during the student protests in England and Wales in 2011, when fourteen police officers were injured, statues in Parliament Square were damaged, windows were smashed and the car that was carrying Prince Charles and his wife Camilla, Duchess of Cornwall was attacked.

The role and influence of the media in the political system

The media plays an important role in informing citizens and influencing the political process in Scotland and the UK, with the majority of the information that the public receives about politics coming from them. This gives the media a great deal of power, as they shape public attitude and opinion. **Free press** means that the media is not censored by the government and can openly criticise it and hold it to account. The media's influence on politics is mainly achieved through newspapers and television; however, the emergence of a sophisticated 'new media' is allowing people to stay abreast of a range of current affairs, including the world of politics.

> ### Key word
> **Free press:** Media that is not censored by the government.

Newspapers

Despite a decline in readership, newspapers remain the traditional medium for information, with 12 million people buying one every day. Most newspapers support a political party and are therefore biased in their reporting of stories. As newspapers are allowed to demonstrate political bias, they are very influential in politics and can persuade people to vote for political parties at election time. They can form a political alliance with a certain party and try to influence voters and shape political attitudes.

The influence of newspapers

Newspapers can be extremely influential in shaping the attitudes of the electorate. For some voters, *The Sun* is their only source of information. This makes the paper extremely powerful and important. In every election since 1992, the party backed by *The Sun* has won the election. In 2010, there was a 5 per cent swing from Labour to the Conservatives among voters; among *The Sun* readers this swing was 13.5 per cent. This paper has also been somewhat influential north of the border. In 2011 the SNP won the first majority government in Scotland with the support of *The Sun*, and this backing may have contributed to the victory. However, it has also been argued that *The Sun* merely backs the party most likely to win the election, according to opinion polls.

Despite a potentially influential role in shaping public attitudes, overall newspaper readership is down: The number of newspapers bought every day is falling and fewer people are buying newspapers today. Especially for younger people, papers are being replaced by newspaper apps, which send news updates, and by newspaper websites. Although newspapers may continue to influence politics in the future, it will most likely be through electronic means rather than in print. Arguably the influence of newspapers on the public is declining.

Television

Unlike newspapers, television must remain politically impartial and cannot support a political party or agenda. Television channels are regulated by Ofcom, which ensures that they are not biased in their reporting. At election time, each political party is given an equal time to deliver a party political broadcast, and therefore television is an influential means through which to inform voters.

The influence of television

Live TV debates were used for the first time in the 2010 Elections. The three main political parties – Labour, Conservatives and Liberal Democrats – all debated live on TV and millions tuned in to each one. Nick Clegg emerged as the 'winner' of these debates, appearing likeable and trustworthy. After the first live debate, support for the Liberal Democrats increased by eleven points – the largest ever increase during an election campaign. In two opinion polls, the Liberal Democrats overtook both Labour and the Conservatives for the first time in 100 years. However, as we know, this did not translate into actual votes at the polls.

Televised leaders' debates also took place before the 2011 Scottish Parliament Election. While Alex Salmond appeared self-assured and confident, the then Labour leader Iain Gray was nervous and tense. However, this did not have the same impact on public opinion as the UK leaders' debates the previous year.

New media

In recent years the internet has become increasingly popular, with an estimated 70 per cent of the public now accessing it on a daily basis. It provides a platform for political parties to reach out to the public and most parties now have websites, Facebook pages, Twitter feeds and YouTube channels. Political parties and politicians are making extensive use of social media to engage voters, especially young people, in politics.

The influence of new media

Newspapers and television continue to have the strongest influence on voting behaviour. In the 2010 General Election, traditional media had the greatest influence on the electorate. The first TV debate was watched by 9.4 million people and *The Sun* newspaper was read by 8 million people every day. By contrast, 79 per cent of people could not recollect any online electioneering.

However, it is widely acknowledged that as new media continues to develop, its influence on politics will become greater. Social media is allowing citizens to become journalists and to participate and interact more than traditional forms of the media allow. Overall, newspapers and television are changing the ways they engage with their readers and viewers. Arguably, this better reflects demands from the electorate, especially the young, and how they access information.

The SNP has, in particular, made effective use of the social media advances sweeping into modern politics and are the trailblazers.

This does not necessarily mean that the SNP is more popular. It may just be that its supporters are more likely to use social media. However, it does ensure that the SNP has a very effective means through which to inform and persuade voters.

Party	Number of Twitter followers
SNP	34,600
Labour	11,100
Greens	8,967
Conservatives	4,592
Liberal Democrats	3,672

Table 4.1 Number of Twitter followers (taken from Scottish political party Twitter pages, July 2014)

Key point

The Leveson Inquiry as an example of the control of the media

In 2012, the Leveson Inquiry was held into the freedom of the press. The Inquiry was set up as a result of allegations of phone hacking from celebrities and members of the public by the now defunct *News of the World*. As a result of the Leveson Inquiry, a Royal Charter was announced to protect the freedom of the press while also protecting the public from the abuses committed by the media prior to the Inquiry.

Figure 4.1 Live TV debates were used for the first time in the 2010 Elections

Chapter 5

Representative democracy in Scotland and the UK

The role of political representatives

The UK is a representative democracy, which means that the electorate votes in elections for the people they want to represent them. These representatives then make decisions on their behalf. MPs and MSPs have both mandatory and discretionary roles and responsibilities that they carry out.

> **Key word**
>
> **Scrutinise:** To examine something closely.

MPs	
Vote in the House of Commons	One of the most important roles of an MP is the power to vote in the House of Commons. Before a bill can be passed as legislation, MPs must individually vote 'Aye' or 'No'. MPs will usually vote in line with their party's wishes but their voting decision should be made on behalf of their constituency. In May 2013 the Marriage (Same Sex Couples) Bill was passed in the Commons by 366 votes to 161 to allow same-sex couples to marry in England and Wales.
Attend adjournment debates	Debates are held in the chamber on a daily basis, providing MPs with the opportunity to represent their constituents in parliament. In debates, the executive is forced to account for its actions. Adjournment debates allow backbench MPs to speak on an issue of importance to their constituents.
Attend Question Time	MPs are given the opportunity to question a government minister on an issue in the House of Commons. This gives MPs the opportunity to **scrutinise** the work of the government. Most of the questions are 'seen' questions, where ministers are allowed to prepare an answer beforehand. The questions are chosen by the Speaker of the House and, as the vast majority are not able to be asked in the allocated time, written answers are given to these instead.
Attend Prime Minister's Questions (PMQs)	PMQs takes place every Wednesday and during this time the prime minister is questioned by MPs about government decisions and current affairs. Although this may not necessarily affect government decision-making, it does affect party popularity and how a leader is viewed.
Membership of committees	Most MPs are members of committees in the House of Commons. Committees give MPs an opportunity to scrutinise the work of the government and influence a specific area of decision-making. Committees reflect the balance of power held in the House of Commons and therefore if a party holds a large majority it can be difficult for the committees effectively to challenge the government. There are different committees in parliament, including Select, Public bills and backbench business committees.
Propose Private Members' Bills	MPs also have the opportunity to propose their own bills. At the beginning of each parliamentary session, twenty applications for Private Members' Bills are selected to be debated for a whole day by the House of Commons. Private Members' Bills rarely reach the later stages of the legislative process.
Undertake constituency work	MPs have important roles and duties that must be carried out in their constituency. The most important role in the constituency is to hold regular surgeries. However, they must also attend meetings in the local community, visit local areas and attend social events and maintain a high profile in the local media.

Table 5.1 The role of an MP

Remember

Reforms have been made to strengthen the effectiveness of UK committees. Chairpersons are now elected by secret ballots, and other members are also chosen by their parties via secret ballots, thus reducing the whips' influence. A backbench business committee determines business before the House on 35 days per session.

MSPs	
Propose motions and debates	MSPs are able to propose motions in parliament. These motions can be about local, national or international issues that affect Scotland. In 2012, Jamie Hepburn MSP proposed a motion calling for the need for an International Arms Trade Treaty.
Attend Question Time	Similar to the system in Westminster, every Thursday morning MSPs participate in a general Question Time whereby government ministers are questioned on their departments. Written questions can also be submitted. Every Thursday afternoon, First Minister's Question Time is held, where the First Minister is questioned on issues.
Join committees	Committees exist to scrutinise the work of the Scottish government and may conduct inquiries into specific areas. In 2012 the Economy, Energy and Tourism Committee conducted an inquiry into the government's green energy target. Donald Trump was called as a witness as he is regarded as an expert on tourism. He gave evidence on the effect of wind farms on tourism. Since 2011, the SNP has had a majority in each of the committees, which has weakened the ability of opposition parties to scrutinise SNP policy. Committees also have the power to propose new bills.
Vote at Decision Time	A further role of MSPs is to vote on issues in parliament. At the end of parliamentary days, MSPs can vote at Decision Time, where votes are passed on any issues debated that day. MSPs are normally instructed how to vote by their political party.

Table 5.2 The role of an MSP

Pressures on representatives

The main role for both MPs and MSPs is to represent constituents. However, as they also remain answerable to their political party, they can find themselves with conflicting pressures. Representatives must try to satisfy their constituents, their party, **whips**, pressure groups and the media, while also upholding their personal beliefs and values. This can result in a range of conflicting loyalties.

Constituency

First and foremost, an MP should represent the constituents who elected them. Obviously it is vital for MPs to placate their constituents given that they may well not be re-elected at the next election.

The political party

Most MPs are elected not for their own personal qualities but because it is believed that they will put into action the policies of their political party. Therefore the MP represents both their constituents and their political party. The MP must remain loyal to their party as they will know that they may only have been elected as a result of their membership to that party.

Key word

Whips: Officials of a political party appointed to maintain parliamentary discipline among its members.

The Party Whip system

To ensure that MPs carry out the wishes of the party, whips are employed to put pressure on the MP to support the party. If an MP votes against the party's wishes, they may be expelled and it will be unlikely that they will be able to gain the necessary public support to be re-elected at the next election.

The role of the legislature

Parliament has two Houses: the House of Commons and the House of Lords. The Commons is the more important of the two as the Lords are un-elected and their powers are limited.

The House of Commons

The House of Commons consists of 650 MPs, each representing a single constituency. MPs consider and propose new laws and can scrutinise government policies by asking ministers questions about current issues, either in the Commons Chamber or in Committees.

House of Commons	
Legislation	All MPs are involved in amending bills and passing laws. One of the main functions of the House of Commons is to legislate. The government will enjoy more power in the House if it has returned a working majority. Thanks to the First Past The Post electoral system, the House is normally controlled by the governing party, which limits the extent to which the government is actually scrutinised by the House of Commons. In August 2013, backbench MPs revolted against their government when 40 coalition MPs went against their chief whip by voting against military action in Syria. MPs are clearly able to influence legislation through their role in the House of Commons.
Committees	Selected MPs sit on committees that are responsible for scrutinising proposed legislation and the work of government departments.
Scrutiny	All MPs are responsible for scrutinising the work of the government through questioning at Question Time and participating in debates.

Table 5.3 The work of the House of Commons

The House of Lords

The House of Lords is the unelected branch of parliament and therefore does not directly represent the people of the UK. Those who are members of the Lords are usually referred to as *peers*.

Although the House of Lords usually gives way to the will of the House of Commons, this branch of the legislature does also carry out a number of roles.

House of Lords	
Debate	Peers in the House of Lords have party affiliations but they tend to be less partisan than MPs in the Commons. Furthermore, they have the opportunity to debate issues in a less politically biased way than the more confrontational House of Commons. It has been argued that legislation is therefore improved by their contributions.
Legislation	Most bills are passed by the House of Lords before becoming law. However, if the House of Lords rejects a non-financial bill that has been passed by the House of Commons in two consecutive parliamentary sessions, it automatically becomes law.
Scrutiny	The House of Lords plays an active role in scrutinising the work of the government, and in some cases it challenges the government's intentions.

Table 5.4 The work of the House of Lords

Remember

The impact and limitations of a coalition government

The House of Lords Reform Bill 2012, which proposed a mainly elected House of Lords, was introduced by Nick Clegg. It became clear that the Government was going to lose the vote on the 'programme motion' and it was later withdrawn. At the vote on whether to give the bill a Second Reading, 91 Conservative MPs voted against the three-line whip, while nineteen more abstained. The Deputy Prime Minister Nick Clegg announced that the Government was abandoning the bill due to the opposition from Conservative backbench MPs, claiming that the Conservatives had 'broken the coalition contract'. In this instance, the existence of a coalition government limited the law-making process in Westminster. As a result, the Liberal Democrats pledged to vote against proposed constituency boundary changes designed to reduce the size of the Commons from 650 to 600 MPs. Again, in September 2014, a Liberal Democrat MP proposed in his Private Members' Bill sweeping exemptions to the 'bedroom tax'. The motion was passed and the bill will move to detailed scrutiny at the committee stage. (The Liberal Democrats, although in Government, now oppose this tax.)

This shows how coalition governments can be a barrier to effective law-making in the UK government when consensus cannot be reached.

The role of the UK and Scottish Executive

The Executive is comprised of the prime minister, the Cabinet and the Civil Service. Unlike the USA, the UK does not have a 'written' Constitution that details the powers of elected representatives. This means that the role of the Executive cannot be found in one single document; instead, the British Constitution is embodied in several documents.

Prime minister	
Leader of the governing party	First and foremost, the PM is the leader of the governing party. They are the person that the public associates with that party. As the leader of the party, it is the PM's responsibility to manage their MPs, and this is achieved through the use of the whip system. Whips have an important role to play, especially in governments with a small majority. It is the whips' job to ensure that every member turns out to vote on the majority votes taking place in parliament. 'Three-line whips' are imposed on significant occasions, such as motions of no confidence.
Appoint Cabinet ministers	The PM is responsible for appointing members to the Cabinet. This is known as the power of **patronage**. Furthermore, the PM is able to reshuffle Cabinet ministers whenever they wish. Most MPs are ambitious and would like to be appointed to the Cabinet and therefore they tend to remain loyal to the party and to their leader. Not only will the PM appoint their allies to the Cabinet, but they may also leave outside the Cabinet those whom they deem to be too powerful.
Appoint peers	The UK honours system allows individuals to be recognised for various achievements and services to their country. Many value the honour of a seat in the House of Lords. The PM has responsibility for appointing many of these honours.

Table 5.5 The role of the prime minister

> **Key word**
>
> **Patronage:** The power to control appointments to particular positions.

First minister	
Leader of the governing party	Like the PM, the first minister is simply the leader of the governing party. As the SNP returned a majority to the Scottish Parliament in 2011, Alex Salmond enjoyed a particularly powerful position regarding the introduction of new laws. As a result, the bills that passed through normally became law, as was the case with the Scottish Independence Referendum Bill (2013).
Powers of patronage	Like the PM, the first minister has powers of patronage – to appoint who they want to the Cabinet. MSPs are appointed by the first minster from their party to run government departments. The first minister must also chair the Cabinet meetings on Wednesday mornings, and they have the power to reshuffle the Cabinet.

Table 5.6 The role of the first minister

The role of the Cabinet

The Cabinet is the ultimate decision-making body of the executive. It is made up of the heads of key departments, legal officers and government whips and headed by the prime minister. The prime minister is supposed to be *primus inter pares* – the first among equals – but some critics have suggested that a more presidential approach has been adopted by recent prime ministers. Cabinet ministers must support all Cabinet decisions and government policy. This is known as **collective responsibility**. Cabinet ministers are held accountable for their department.

Similarly, the Scottish Cabinet comprises MSPs selected by the first minister to run certain departments. The Scottish Cabinet normally meets weekly at Bute House in Edinburgh, and also operates on the basis of collective responsibility.

The role of the Civil Service

Within the Executive branch there is a non-political or a neutral element known as the Civil Service. While government ministers make the policy, civil servants administer those decisions. Unlike politicians who are elected to their positions, civil servants are permanent appointees who are not responsible for the success or failure of departments. As civil servants can remain in departments for many years, unlike elected ministers, they can acquire expert knowledge in certain areas. The Civil Service is a matter reserved to UK Parliament and therefore the Civil Service in Scotland remains part of the Home Civil Service. However, Scottish civil servants are accountable to Scottish ministers, who are themselves accountable to the Scottish Parliament.

> ## Key word
>
> **Collective responsibility:** All decisions reached by ministers, individually or collectively, are binding on all members of the government.

> ## Remember
>
> Scotland, unlike Westminster, has only one chamber. This means that legislation does not go to a revising chamber for amendments. This, therefore, reduces the extent to which the actions of the government can be checked and balanced. The Scottish Government since 2011 has been able to take executive action and legislate without the risk of defeat.

Opportunities to scrutinise the respective Executives

UK Parliament

- Votes in the House of Commons can give backbench MPs the opportunity to rebel. In October 2013, a total of 81 of David Cameron's MPs voted for a Commons motion calling for a referendum on Britain's relationship with the EU, even though the Prime Minister had ordered his party to oppose it.
- Prime Minister's Question Time gives MPs from both the governing and the opposition parties the ability to question the prime minister. Prime Minister's Question Time may not necessarily affect policy but it does change the way that a party is viewed by the electorate.
- Select Committees scrutinise the work of the government. Membership of committees reflects party strength and so they are dominated by the governing party, which can limit the ability of the opposition party to hold the Executive to account.

- Opposition Days are set aside as an opportunity for opposition parties to criticise government policy. Opposition parties generally use these as opportunities to try to embarrass the Executive.
- The House of Lords effectively challenges the Executive and limits its power. As Lords are unelected, this challenge is more effective because they are more independent than MPs. Furthermore, most have already enjoyed a political career and so are not influenced by the prospect of career advancements from the prime minister.

Scottish Parliament

- Much like in Westminster, voting in the Scottish parliament allows the legislative to limit the power of the Executive. However, as a result of the SNP majority Government elected in 2011, the extent to which opposition parties can prevent the government from being too powerful has been limited. In 2012 the Scotland Act was passed, which allowed the Scottish Government to hold the 2014 referendum on Scottish Independence.
- Similarly, while Committees offer opportunities to ensure a balance of power, they have been dominated by the SNP since the last election and have therefore had a limited ability to hold the Executive to account.
- First Minister's Question Time gives MSPs from the governing and opposition parties the chance to question the government on its actions. This can have an effect on the way in which the first minister and their party are viewed.

These methods all ensure that both the UK and Scottish Executives do not hold too much power and that there remains a balance of power between the legislature and the Executive.

Question and model answer

Question ❓

One aim of an electoral system is to provide fair representation.

Evaluate the effectiveness of an electoral system you have studied in providing fair representation.

You should refer to the electoral system used in Scotland or the United Kingdom or both in your answer. **12 marks**

Responses will be credited that make reference to:

- the main features of an electoral system
- an evaluation of the success of the electoral system in providing for fair representation.

Up to **8 marks** for knowledge (description, explanation and exemplification) and up to **4 marks** for evaluative comments.

Remember 📌

Knowledge questions will have either 12 or 20 marks allocated and you will answer one question from a choice of two. If an answer contains more analytical/ evaluative points than are required to gain the allocation of 4 marks, these can be credited as knowledge and understanding marks.

Model answer

Additional Member System (AMS) is used to elect MSPs to the Scottish Parliament. AMS is a mixture of FPTP to elect constituency MSPs and PR to elect regional list MSPs. It could therefore be argued that AMS is fairer as it provides broader representation because the electorate have two votes: More Parties gain fairer representation through the party list for example in Glasgow the Greens and the Conservatives each gained a seat. So all those who voted for these parties were rewarded and this will encourage them to vote in the next election. In contrast FPTP system is 'winner-takes-all system'.

AMS is fairer because it reduces the gap between % of votes and percentage of seats. In 2011, Conservatives gained about 13% of the votes and received almost 12% of the seats which is clearly proportional. Whereas in the 2010 General election in Scotland, Conservatives received almost 17% of the Scottish vote yet achieved only one MP less than 2% of the seats. So AMS is clearly a fairer system for the Conservatives.

Under AMS, smaller Parties are better represented which is fairer. In 2007, the Greens and SSP gained 13 out of 50 regional seats in the Scottish Parliament. However by the 2011 Scottish parliament election only three MSPs were not from the three major parties. So this weakens the argument that AMS is fairer as it provides appropriate representation for minority parties.

It is also claimed that AMS provides better representation for women and ethnic minorities than FPTP. Women make up 35% of MSPs with 45 being elected in 2012. In contrast only 23% of MPs are women so AMS is fairer. However Ethnic Minority representation in the Scottish parliament is not fair. In the 1999 and 2003 Scottish elections no Ethnic Minority MPs were elected and unfortunately the one MP from an Ethnic Minority elected in 2007 died. It is correct that in 2011 two Ethnic Minority MPs were elected but they are still under-represented with less than 2% of the MSPs. In contrast Ethnic Minority MPs total 27 in the UK Parliament double the Scottish percentage. However the percentage of Ethnic Minorities in England is double that of Scotland's.

Under AMS, a coalition is usually formed and whilst this may be more proportional, it must be remembered that no-one voted for a coalition. Between 1999–2007 the Liberal Democrats were part of the coalition government with Labour and this meant that the majority of voters were represented. However was it fair that the second largest party the SNP were excluded from government?

Overall it is clear that AMS is a far fairer system than FPTP despite its poor record on ethnic minority representation. Voters have greater choice and there is not a massive difference between votes cast and seats gained which is the hallmark of fairness.

Marker's comment

This is an excellent answer because it is rich in *knowledge* and *evaluation*. Each point is fully explained, with examples where possible. The candidate examines a range of issues that are relevant to the question and provides up-to-date evidence to support the view of fair representation. This answer also provides balance by offering counter-arguments that are relevant and insightful. The conclusion considers the extent to which the view is supported. This answer would gain full marks. **12/12**

Part Three: Social issues in the UK

This section of the book provides summary course notes for the Social Issues in the UK unit of the course.

You will have studied one of the following topics as part of your CfE Higher Social Issues unit:

- Social Inequality
- Crime and the Law

In the extended response/essay section of the exam, you will answer either a 12-mark question or a 20-mark question.

Chapter 6
Social inequality

What you should know 👍

SQA requirements

To be successful in this section, you should know about:

★ the evidence of social inequality
★ social explanations/theories and causes of social inequality
★ the impact of social inequality and government responses
★ the impact of social inequality and government responses: case study on health
★ the impact of social inequality and government responses: case study on gender and ethnic minorities.

Evidence of social inequality

Poverty

The UK and Scottish governments define poverty by relating it to a household's income. You are considered to be living in **relative poverty** if your income is less than 60 per cent of the UK average income. This 'poverty line' stood at £317 per week in 2012 for a household with two adults and two children under 13.

Key words

Absolute poverty: Not having the things an individual needs to survive, for example food, clothing, shelter and energy.

Relative poverty: Households whose income is less than 60 per cent of average incomes in the UK.

Classifications and causes of poverty

- **Persistent poverty:** Where someone experiences long periods of poverty, possibly due to long-term unemployment. Once trapped in poverty, families can spend generations within the poverty trap. Some 3.7 million working-age households have no one in employment (18 per cent of total households).
- **Recurrent poverty:** Many occupations are cyclical in nature. Those working in outdoor activities such as skiing may find that during the summer months they experience poverty.

- **The impact of the world banking crisis of 2008 and government spending cuts:** According to the Joseph Rowntree Foundation, the average incomes of the lowest social groups known as DE, have fallen by 8 per cent since 2008.
- **The gap between the costs of essentials and real wages is widening:** According to a Joseph Rowntree Foundation report in June 2014, the bills for what the public considers basic necessities have soared 28 per cent since 2008, while average earnings have increased by 9 per cent.

A June 2014 report by the Poverty Action Group stated that people were being blamed for being poor and it was assumed that they were work shy. The reality is that more than half of Scots suffering poverty and **social exclusion** live in working households trapped in low-paid jobs and zero-hours contracts. This contradicts the UK Government's view that 'work is the best route out of poverty'. According to the Joseph Rowntree Foundation, an adult working a 40-hour week on the minimum wage will earn £1027 a month, or £12,334 annually, in pre-tax income. According to the Joseph Rowntree Foundation, however, a single person now needs to earn at least £14,400 a year to reach a 'minimum income standard' and afford a socially acceptable standard of living.

Key word

Social exclusion: The impact of poverty on individuals and groups and the extent to which they are unable to participate in aspects of society, for example education, health and housing, due to being in poverty.

Groups at risk of social exclusion

- Those with low levels of skills due to poor education.
- Unemployment or low-paid work may result in some people not being able to participate in social networks, such as membership of exercise clubs or activity groups.
- Children from lower income backgrounds may not be able to participate in many activities, such as school trips or after-school clubs. This can affect their self-esteem and contribute towards the cycle of poverty.
- Disability and long-term ill-health are also more likely to result in social exclusion as there is less access to employment and increased living costs.
- Elderly people who depend totally on the state pension can struggle to cover rising living costs and experience fuel poverty.
- Women are generally at a higher risk of poverty as they are more likely to be involved in unpaid care, to be in lower paid employment or part-time work and tend to have lower pensions.
- Ethnic minority groups may experience social exclusion due to discrimination, racism and poor housing.

Are welfare reforms a cause of poverty?

According to a June 2014 report by the Welfare Reform Committee of the Scottish Parliament, the answer is 'Yes'. Welfare reforms will take £1.6 billion from the Scottish economy. Those who live in the most deprived communities of Scotland will suffer the most. The impact of welfare reforms on wealthy St Andrews will amount to £180 annually for each adult aged between 16 and 64, while the equivalent figure in Calton in the east end of Glasgow is £880.

John Dickie of Child Poverty Action Group stated: 'These unprecedented cuts are not only damaging families and undermining children's well-being, they are robbing local business of much-needed income and storing up huge costs in the long term as we try and fix the health, educational and social damage that poverty causes.'

Further evidence had been provided by the Scottish Government 2012–13 Annual Poverty and Income Inequality in Scotland Report (published in July 2014). The Report stated that 820,000 people were now classified as living in poverty in Scotland, with the number of children in poverty increasing by 30,000. The Report blamed the reform of the benefits system, tightening of eligibility for tax credits and stagnating wages.

However, the UK Government disagrees and argues that welfare reforms are helping the poor. A Department for Work and Pensions spokesperson stated: 'The truth is that employment is up and unemployment is falling and our vital reforms are working. We are returning fairness to the welfare system and helping people lift themselves out of poverty by making work pay. We are transforming the lives of the poorest people in society … keeping the benefits bill sustainable, so we can support people when they need it most.'

Food banks

The 2014 Charity Report stated that the need for food banks is a national disgrace. The report 'Below the Breadline', produced by Church Action on Poverty, the Trussell Trust and Oxfam, charts the dramatic rise in need for food parcels. In 2012 more than 13 million meals were given out across the UK, and this figure increased to over 20 million in 2013.

Oxfam Scotland stated: 'Food banks provide invaluable support for families on the breadline, but the fact they are needed in Scotland in the twenty-first century is a stain on our national conscience. Too many people need more help to deal with the consequences of stagnating wages, insecure work and rising food and fuel prices.'

Figure 6.1 A food bank in Scotland

Impact of social inequality on selected groups

Elderly people

The proportion of pensioners living in low-income households (after housing costs are deducted) has fallen sharply from 26 per cent of all pensioners in 2001–02 to 14 per cent in 2011–12.

In 2013, it was estimated that 1.8 million elderly people were living below the official poverty line. Of that figure, 1 million lived in severe poverty (defined as below 50 per cent of the average income after housing costs).

In the UK, about one-third of all pensioner households entitled to pension credit are not claiming it – equivalent to 1.3 million households. This explains why pressure groups are against **means-tested benefits** for elderly people.

Cost	Benefit
£2 billion	Winter Fuel Payment of £200 per household/ £300 for over-80s
£1 billion	Free bus passes in England and Wales
£600 million	Free television licences for over-80s

Table 6.1 The cost of benefits for elderly people

Views of organisations

'We strongly oppose any move to more means-testing of older people. It leaves out many people who need money but do not claim, and it is complex, inefficient and costly in terms of administration. Worse still, it penalises those who have saved, whereas **universal benefits** are straightforward and ensure all those who need them receive what they should.'

Saga (pressure group for elderly people)

'It is very noticeable that wealthy pensioners arc the one group that have not been affected by the austerity programme as a whole.'

Institute of Fiscal Studies

Key words

Means-tested benefits: A person must be on a low or designated income before the entitled benefit is received, for example child benefit.

Universal benefits: Individuals receive the entitled benefits regardless of their income, for example state pensions and free prescriptions (excluding England).

Fuel poverty

The official definition of 'fuel poverty' is when a household must pay more than 10 per cent of its disposable income to heat their home to an adequate level. Since 2010 it is estimated energy prices have increased by 37 per cent, and this has led to dramatic increases in fuel poverty.

Child poverty

Poverty has a devastating effect on children growing up. It affects their whole life, from health and wellbeing to educational attainment and aspirations.

There were 3.5 million children living in poverty in the UK in 2014: 27 per cent of children, or more than one in four. At a local level, statistics are even more concerning in some areas. In the Calton area of Glasgow, 49 per cent of children live in poverty. In Glasgow, Manchester and Liverpool, approximately one-third of all children live below the poverty line.

Child poverty in the UK: Facts and figures

- 3.5 million (27 per cent) of children live in poverty in the UK, which in 2012 was at its lowest level in 25 years. It peaked in the 1990s at 34 per cent.
- Child poverty fell by 9.9 per cent in Scotland between 2001 and 2011, compared with 5.7 per cent in England. Child poverty is projected to rise with an expected 600,000 more children living in poverty by 2016.
- Babies from disadvantaged families are more likely to be born underweight – an average of 200 grams lower than babies from the richest families.
- Children from low-income households are nearly three times more likely to suffer mental health problems than children from more affluent households.
- Children living in poverty are almost twice as likely to live in bad housing. This has significant effects on both their physical and mental health, as well as their educational achievement.
- Children who are from socially deprived backgrounds are more likely to be obese due to a poor diet of junk food and cheap ready meals.

Social inequality and education

Children growing up in poorer families leave school with substantially lower levels of educational attainment. This begins in primary 1, where pupils from a deprived background can be up to a year behind their middle-class counterparts developmentally, and lack basic skills such as problem-solving and literacy. In 2013, in Scotland as a whole, just 2.5 per cent of the 8872 fifth-year students who came from the bottom 20 per cent of households achieved three As or more in their Higher exams.

Entry to higher education is barred to many students, especially in England and Wales. Annual fees of between £6000 and £9000 are now allowed, and over half of universities in England charge the maximum fee. In contrast, university education in Scotland is free to all Scottish students, as fees are paid for by the Scottish government. Again in Scotland, young people from low-income families at school and college can claim the Education Maintenance Allowance (EMA), which was scrapped in England by the Coalition Government.

However, Scottish universities, especially St Andrew's, have been criticised for not admitting enough students from poorer backgrounds. The Scottish government has responded to the worrying statistics of low admittance of poor students by increasing funding to universities that admit pupils from poorer backgrounds. Following 'outcome agreements', universities will have to admit more pupils from poorer backgrounds to receive the additional funding. This has led Edinburgh University to agree to increase its student numbers from the poorest areas by 50 per cent, or an extra 45 places.

Positive discrimination

Students who apply to Glasgow University from areas of multiple deprivation can be provided with reduced exam requirements for entry to their course. This is to compensate for the disadvantages that they face growing up. Critics have argued that the universities are 'dumbing down' academic integrity. However, research indicates that these students do just as well as those accepted with higher grades.

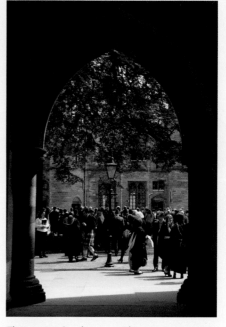

Figure 6.2 Students at Glasgow University

Unemployed young adults

The unemployment rate for 16- to 24-year-olds is now more than four times the rate of older workers. The unemployment rate among 16- and 17-year-olds is 36 per cent, and 18 per cent among 18- to 24-year-olds. This compares to 4.7 per cent among 35- to 49-year-olds. Unemployment of young people, especially in cities, can lead to a host of major societal issues, for example poverty, social exclusion, drug abuse and crime, and their related impacts on the individual's physical and mental wellbeing. Former Prime Minister Tony Blair stated: 'a big cause of the riots in England in 2011 was an alienated, disaffected youth ... outside the social mainstream'.

Government responses to social inequality

The Welfare State

The Welfare State is a product of post-war Britain and exists to provide social care from the cradle to the grave. The Labour Government implemented the principles of the Beveridge Report to provide a safety net for all citizens based on the main principles of equality and collectivism. The National Health Service was set up, state education expanded and a social security system to protect elderly, disabled and unemployed people.

Beveridge's five 'giant evils' in society

- **Want:** A reformed social security system would provide every citizen with their basic financial needs.
- **Ignorance:** Education would be reformed so that every child would gain a worthwhile level of education.
- **Squalor:** A massive rebuilding of safer and progressive housing would ensure better living standards for all.
- **Idleness:** A reformed economic policy including the nationalisation of industries such as railways, gas and electricity would ensure low levels of unemployment.
- **Disease:** A new National Health Service that would be free at the point of entry would be created for everyone's health needs.

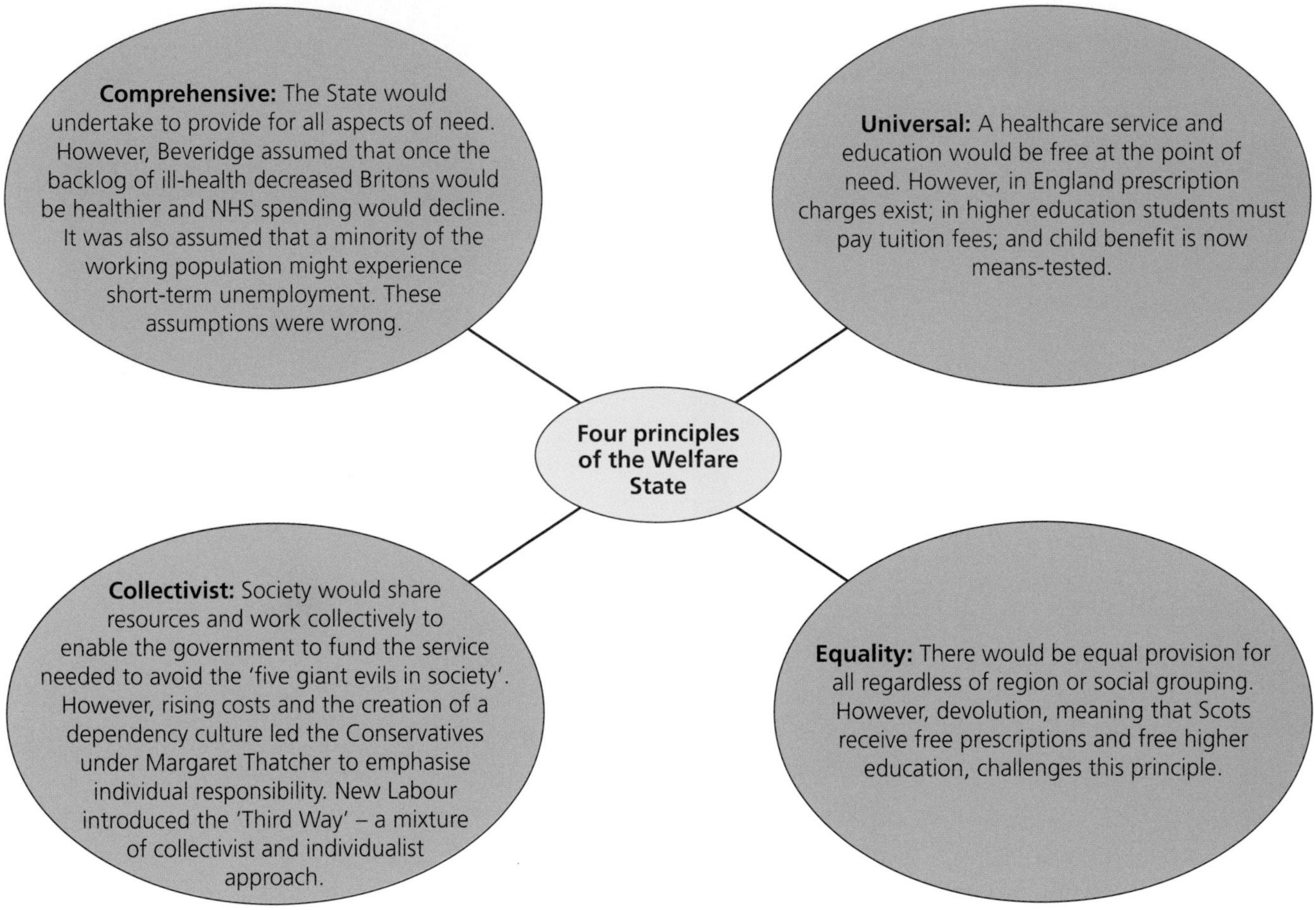

Comprehensive: The State would undertake to provide for all aspects of need. However, Beveridge assumed that once the backlog of ill-health decreased Britons would be healthier and NHS spending would decline. It was also assumed that a minority of the working population might experience short-term unemployment. These assumptions were wrong.

Universal: A healthcare service and education would be free at the point of need. However, in England prescription charges exist; in higher education students must pay tuition fees; and child benefit is now means-tested.

Four principles of the Welfare State

Collectivist: Society would share resources and work collectively to enable the government to fund the service needed to avoid the 'five giant evils in society'. However, rising costs and the creation of a dependency culture led the Conservatives under Margaret Thatcher to emphasise individual responsibility. New Labour introduced the 'Third Way' – a mixture of collectivist and individualist approach.

Equality: There would be equal provision for all regardless of region or social grouping. However, devolution, meaning that Scots receive free prescriptions and free higher education, challenges this principle.

Figure 6.3 The four principles of the Welfare State

Strategies to increase levels of employment

National Minimum Wage (NMW)

The NMW was introduced in April 1999 and in 2014 it was set at £6.50 an hour for those aged 21 and over. Over 1 million workers benefit from it, especially low-paid women workers. The Low Pay Commission Report 2014 claims that the NMW applies to over 1.3 million workers and that it has reduced the gender inequality gap, as women account for 59 per cent of low-paid jobs and therefore benefit from the NMW.

Campaign for a living wage

With the increase of working families experiencing financial hardship, it is clear that the NMW does not give families financial security. The Living Wage Foundation has campaigned tirelessly to encourage employers to offer a living wage rather than the basic NMW. It is estimated that nearly 600 employers across Scotland and the UK have now signed a commitment to provide a living wage of £8.80 per hour for those living in London and £7.65 per hour for the rest of the UK.

New Deal

The New Labour Government introduced the New Deal for Lone Parents (NDLP) as part of its package to address inequality in the UK. New Deal also has programmes for other groups including New Deal for Young People (NDYP), New Deal 25+ and New Deal 50. The New Deal ended in 2011.

Tax credits

The Labour Government of 1997 had a long-term goal to halve child poverty by 2010 and abolish it within a generation. Working tax credits and child tax credits were central to this strategy. The lower the income, the more tax credits individuals and families received. These credits were designed to tackle child poverty and help to ensure that work paid more than welfare. Since 2011, the number of individuals and families receiving credits and the amount received has been reduced.

Jobseeker's Allowance

The Jobseeker's Allowance was introduced in 1996 to replace Unemployment Benefit and is available for those seeking work. At the Jobcentre, a 'Claimant Commitment' is drawn up that sets out the steps that need to be taken to find work. If a claimant fails to carry out the details in the agreement then their benefits can be stopped.

Jobcentre Plus

Jobcentre Plus is a government agency that supports people of working age to move from welfare to work and helps employers to fill their vacancies; it also helps to provide opportunities for retraining and gaining more skills to increase the likelihood of people entering employment. The *Universal Jobsmatch* website is the busiest recruitment website in the UK, with up to 6 million hits per day. In addition to helping people find work, the website allows the government Department for Work and Pensions to track users' attempts to gain employment, and those claiming Jobseeker's Allowance can have their payments stopped if they are not sufficiently active.

Pension credit

Pension credit is a means-tested benefit for elderly people on low incomes, who may depend only on their state pension. All pensioners, regardless of income, receive the Winter Fuel Payment of £200 per household; however, the Cold Weather Payment is means-tested. A new state pension system will be introduced in 2016.

Reasons for the Coalition's welfare revolution

Economic

The Coalition Government agreed to make £81 billion in public spending savings by 2015 as a response to the economic crisis of 2008–10. The welfare budget was no longer affordable: overall spending on benefits was three times bigger in real terms than it was in the late 1970s.

Public support

The Conservative slogan that the system should reward 'strivers not skivers' met with general approval.

Tackling the dependency culture

Those out of work represent a drain on public finances and so getting people into work and contributing to the economy was regarded as the best solution to reduce the public deficit.

Over-complicated system

The Coalition Government intends to simplify the system by amalgamating a number of working-age benefits and tax credits into one single monthly payment, called **Universal Credit**. The Government claims the changes will be cheaper to administer, improve incentives to work, reduce fraud and encourage those on benefits to display greater financial responsibility.

Encourage individual responsibility

Housing benefit, for example, will no longer be paid directly to the landlord but to the claimant as part of their Universal Credit monthly payment. The claimant will be expected to manage their budget and pay their landlord themselves.

> **Key word**
>
> **Universal Credit:** A new payment will simplify the benefits system by combining income-based Jobseeker's Allowance, Employment and Support Allowance, housing benefits and Working and Child Tax Credits into one monthly payment.

Factfile: Key welfare changes, 2013–14

End of Child Benefit as a universal benefit

Families earning £60,000 or more on an individual salary will no longer receive Child Benefit. This policy has been criticised for penalising stay-at-home mothers: A family with four children and one salary of £60,000 will receive *no* Child Benefit. In contrast, a two-income family with a combined income of £100,000 will still receive *full* Child Benefit!

End of the spare-room subsidy

More commonly referred to as the 'bedroom tax', this policy was introduced to address some of the shortages of social housing. Its aim was to encourage those living in large houses to downsize and so reduce waiting times for larger families to find suitable accommodation. A reduction in housing benefit of 14 per cent for those with one spare bedroom and 25 per cent for those with two or more spare bedrooms has been implemented. However, there is a shortage of available homes for people to move to and the reduction of benefits paid to vulnerable people in society has had a detrimental impact on their lives.

In May 2014 it was announced that the 'bedroom tax' would be scrapped in Scotland after the Coalition Government agreed to give Scottish ministers full powers to compensate the 70,000 Scottish households affected by this policy.

Annual increase to benefits capped

From April 2013, increases to benefits excluding state pensions were capped at 1 per cent. The Government justification was that those in work were receiving no or limited wage rises and it was unfair that unemployed people should receive higher benefit increases.

Universal Credit and Help to Work

Claimants who are unemployed for more than two years and who have been unsuccessful in the Work Programme will be enrolled in the Help to Work scheme and offered casual contracted work, also known as 'zero-hours contracts'. Should a claimant refuse these offers without any good reason, they will incur financial penalties.

Personal Independence Payment (PIP) and Work Capability Assessment (WCA)

Previously known as the Disability Living Allowance (DLA), the PIP is a payment given to people living with long-term illnesses or disabilities. The Work Capability Assessment (WCA) is applicable to anyone receiving Incapacity Benefit, Severe Disablement Allowance and Income Support paid on the grounds of illness or disability. Claimants will now be individually assessed, where previously they would only require a doctor's certificate. The assessments are carried out by a private firm.

In 2014 it was reported that between August 2010 and June 2013, 158,300 people with disabilities or a serious illness were assessed by ATOS as fit for work.

Individual benefits cap

Applied through Universal Credit, the cap is £2,167 a month for joint claimants and single claimants with children, and £1,517 a month for a single claimant with no dependent children. This roughly equates to no more than £26,000 in benefits annually.

The Claimant Commitment and Work Programme

The Claimant Commitment replaces the Jobseeker's Agreement. Out-of-work people who break the agreed commitment face financial sanctions. In 2013 almost 900,000 sanctions were imposed on unemployed Scots. One man had his benefits reduced to £11 a week when he failed to attend an interview with a Work Programme, despite producing a doctor's certificate to say he had been diagnosed with terminal cancer and was not fit to travel.

The Work Programme requires those who have been unemployed for more than twelve months to enter on to a special programme in which private and voluntary companies, together with Jobcentre Plus, work to get claimants into long-term and sustained employment. This scheme replaces the New Deal and Pathways to Employment.

The Scottish dimension

The SNP Government supports universal benefits and provides a collectivist, rather than an individualist, approach to the Welfare State. Free prescriptions and free eye tests exist in Scotland but not in England. However, Johann Lamont, the former Scottish Labour Leader, has questioned the affordability of these benefits, along with free university places for Scottish students. With £3.3 billion of cuts being imposed on the Scottish budget, she argued for the end of a 'something for nothing culture' and for a review of all universal benefits.

Social inequality and health

Despite the achievements of the NHS, there is clear evidence that a person's social position, gender, ethnic origin and the area in which they live can affect their chances of achieving good health. One school of thought argues that poverty is the most crucial factor related to health and cites numerous reports to support this viewpoint. Their solution is a collectivist approach to tackling the social and economic impact of social exclusion. In contrast, the individualist approach states that all citizens have access to the NHS and must take responsibility for their own health; that obesity, smoking and the over-consumption of alcohol are lifestyle choices.

Geographic inequalities

There is a clear north–south divide in the health of the British public. Life expectancy for men is lower in Scotland than in England: 75.8 compared to 78.0.

However, there are areas in Scotland and northern England that compare favourably with the healthiest areas in the south-east of England, while parts of London have poor health comparable with the most deprived areas in the country. It is clear that social class and lifestyle play a crucial role.

Evidence of the link between poverty and poor health

The Black Report 1980

Numerous reports have highlighted the link between poverty and poor health. The first and therefore the most famous was the Black Report in 1980. This enquiry into inequalities in health established for the first time a clear link between socio-economic groups and health.

The Acheson Report 1998

This Report provided a comprehensive survey of the condition of disadvantaged people, and its conclusion echoed the Black Report – that poverty had to be tackled through concerted government action and a policy of social inclusion in education, housing, employment, social services and health provision.

CACI Report 2006

The CACI Report highlighted the north–south health divide and confirmed the shockingly unhealthy lifestyles of a significant number of Scots (Scottish regions account for 22 out of the top 25 UK illness areas). The Report found that Scots are more likely to suffer long-term illness, take less exercise, be more overweight and spend more on cigarettes and alcohol than other Britons.

WHO Report 2008

The World Health Organization Report concluded that 'social injustice is killing people on a grand scale', for instance a boy in the Calton district of Glasgow's East End is likely to live to 54, but just a few miles away in the prosperous suburb of Lenzie, average male life expectancy rises to 82.

Scottish Government Report 2013

This Report stated that boys and girls born in the most affluent areas of Scotland in 2011–12 can hope to reach the age of 70 and 72 before suffering poor health. In contrast, boys in the poorest areas will only reach 46.

Office for National Statistics (ONS) 2014

This Report revealed that only three-quarters of boys and 85 per cent of girls born in Glasgow will reach their 65th birthday. The average life expectancy of babies born in the city was 72.6 years for boys and 78.5 years for girls – eight to ten years behind the best-performing areas in the UK.

The biology of poverty

Harry Burns, the former chief medical officer for Scotland, referred to the west of Scotland as experiencing a 'biology of poverty'. The collapse of heavy industry, generations of male unemployment and a breakdown in family and community relationships has affected generations of children and created a cycle of entrapment.

Three Cities Report 2010

This research examined the health and death rates of the citizens of Glasgow, Manchester and Liverpool between 2003 and 2007 – cities with broadly similar deprivation figures. Yet:

- there are 900 extra deaths per year in Glasgow compared to Manchester and Liverpool
- Glasgow's cancer and heart disease deaths are well above those of Manchester and Liverpool
- more disturbing are the alcohol- and drugs-related deaths in Glasgow – more than double the figures of the other two cities.

Lifestyle issues

Individualists argue that although social inequality can be a factor, it is bad lifestyle choices that create poor health, as indicated in Figure 6.4. However, this view is challenged by those who argue that social inequality has a detrimental impact on lifestyle choices and quality of life: living in a damp home surrounded by a drab and depressing environment, with limited life opportunities and choices, has a negative effect on health.

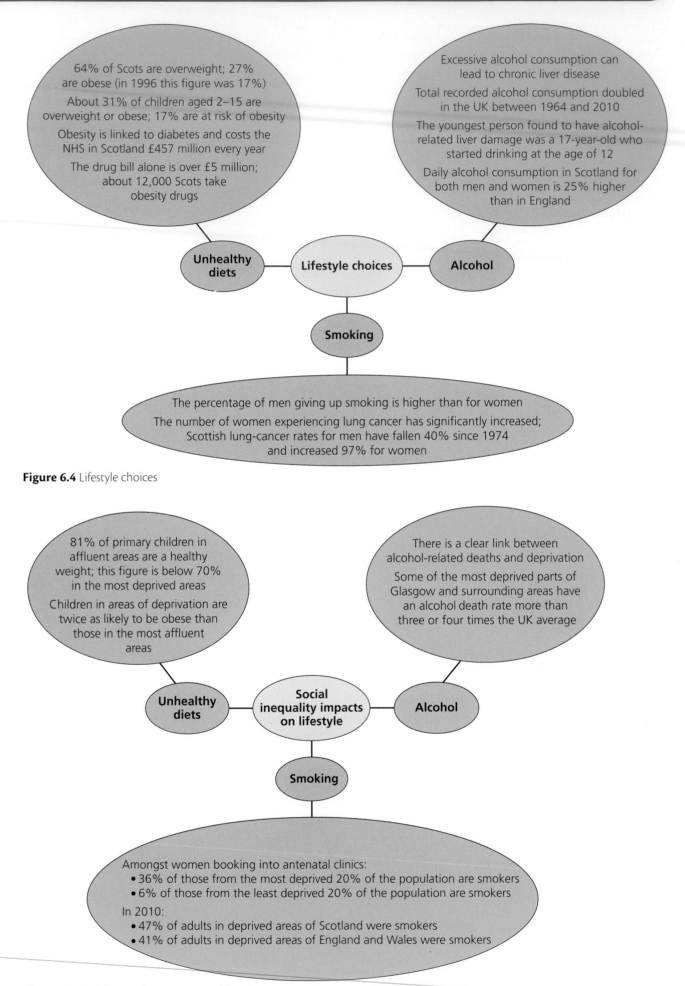

Figure 6.4 Lifestyle choices

Figure 6.5 Social inequality impacts on lifestyle

Government responses to health inequalities

Health is a devolved issue and both the Labour/Liberal Democrats and SNP Governments have tried to improve the health of the Scottish people and to reduce health inequalities.

Key initiatives

Increased UK and Scottish spending on health

In England, health spending rose from £34 billion in 1998 to £90 billion in 2008–09; and in Scotland from £4.6 million to £10.3 million in the same period. Since 2010, the austerity cuts have been less severe for the NHS than for other services, such as education. However, the health service is struggling to cope with an ageing population and the rise of obesity and its associated illnesses.

Free prescriptions and eye tests in Scotland

In 2011, Scotland followed the example of Wales and introduced free prescriptions. Nicola Sturgeon, then Deputy First Minister, stated: 'Prescription charges are a tax on ill health, and can be a barrier to good health for too many people. This Scottish Government is committed to building a healthier nation; through tackling the health inequalities that still scar our nation and supporting people to live longer and lead healthier lives.' However, Scottish Labour and the Scottish Conservatives are opposed to free prescriptions.

Measures to reduce smoking

In 2006 in Scotland and in 2007 in England, smoking was banned in public places. Other actions put in place banned tobacco sales from vending machines and raised the legal age for buying tobacco from 16 to 18. Under proposed 2014–15 legislation, motorists would be banned from smoking in their cars if children were passengers.

Measures to tackle obesity

UK and Scottish government health campaigns have raised awareness. The most recent was in July 2014, urging parents to give water rather than sugary drinks to their children. The *Sunday Herald*, with the support of the medical profession, launched a campaign to persuade retailers not to sell high-energy drinks such as Red Bull to children under 16.

Hungry for Success campaigns in schools have been introduced to promote healthy eating. Alex Salmond announced that free school meals would be provided from January 2015 for all primary 1–3 pupils (this was introduced in England in August 2014).

The 2013 Scottish Health Survey found that these measures were working: the proportion of boys with a weight problem had fallen from 38 per cent to 31 per cent – a significant improvement.

Tackling alcohol abuse

In June 2012, the Alcohol (Minimum Pricing Scotland) Act was passed, which the Scottish Government hopes will eventually lead to the introduction of a minimum price of 50p per unit of alcohol. However, opposition from the Scottish Whiskey Industry, which has appealed to the European Union, has delayed the implementation of the policy.

Tackling poverty and poor health

The Scottish Government strategy to tackle income inequality and health inequality is set out in the 2008 *Equally Well Report*; an extract appears to the right.

Overview of health improvements

The health of all citizens is improving, including those in areas of deprivation. The gap in life expectancy between the best and worst parts of the UK has fallen from 10.6 years to 10.3 for men and from 9.2 years to 8.1 years for women since 2000–02. According to the 2012 Scottish Household Survey, more than 200,000 Scots have given up smoking over the last ten years, death rates from coronary heart disease have significantly fallen and life expectancy has increased. However, significant health inequalities still exist and the cuts in public expenditure could once again widen the health division.

Characteristics of policies more likely to be effective in reducing inequalities in health:

- structural changes in the environment (e.g. installing affordable heating in damp, cold houses)
- legislative and regulatory controls (e.g. smoking bans in workplaces)
- fiscal policies (e.g. increasing the price of tobacco and alcohol products)
- reducing price barriers (e.g. free prescriptions)
- starting young (e.g. prenatal and postnatal support and interventions, home visits to infants, good quality pre-school day care).

Social inequality: gender and ethnicity

Both women and people from ethnic minorities have made progress towards greater equality in the workplace through legislation and changing attitudes, but much has still to be done.

The glass ceiling

Despite more women going through higher education than men, women still lag behind men in income earnings and in promotion. The term 'glass ceiling' is used to describe how women and other disadvantaged groups are restricted in their ability to climb the promotion ladder; it usually refers to barriers to senior management. The Ambition and Gender at Work report by the Institute of Leadership and Management found that 73 per cent of women felt that barriers still exist for those seeking senior management and board-level positions.

Perhaps the biggest reason for a lack of women in top senior positions is the culture of 'presenteeism' that exists within UK businesses. Many senior managers are expected to work long hours. There is a real lack of flexible and part-time working arrangements in senior positions.

Women and inequality

Women have lower pay

- lower pay for the same work
- work in lower-paid sectors of the economy
- interrupted employment
- part-time work

Women take greater responsibility for family and caring

- make up over 90% of lone parents
- bear a greater burden of the cost of children

The gender pay gap varies from industry to industry, with the biggest differential being in banking and finance where men earn 44 per cent more than women.

Women are over-represented in areas of the economy that are low paid. Nearly two-thirds of women are employed in twelve occupation groups, sometime described as the five Cs: caring, cashiering, catering, cleaning and clerical occupations.

Part-time work

Many more women than men work part time. Women are most likely to work part time when they are caring for young children. Approximately two-thirds of women with children under the age of eleven work part time, compared to only one-third of women with no dependent children.

The impact of government public sector cuts

One of the Coalition's economic policies has been to reduce the number of public-sector workers while at the same time encouraging growth in the private sector. This strategy has had a detrimental impact on employment opportunities for women. The Fawcett Society and the Scottish Close the Gap project highlight that since 2010 three times as many women as men have become unemployed in the long term: 103,000 women compared to 37,000 men.

Lone parents

Perhaps the greatest reason that women face huge inequalities is the impact that being a lone parent has on employment. In the UK, 25 per cent of families are lone-parent families, which equates to 1.7 million parents with 2.9 million dependent children. Nine out of ten lone parents are lone mothers.

Figure 6.6 Single-parent families are more likely to live in poverty than families with two parents

When lone parents find work it is often low paid, so they merely replace workless poverty with working poverty; lone parents have a high risk of living in poverty whether or not they are in work. According to research, nearly 86 per cent of working households that are in poverty are lone-parent households.

Progress and limitations

- Numbers of women are growing in occupations previously dominated by men. Women now account for 75 per cent of pharmacists, 33 per cent of medical practitioners, nearly half of all lawyers and almost 40 per cent of all accountants.
- The proportion of female managers and senior officials increased from less than 10 per cent in the early 1990s to more than one-third in recent times. Therefore, increasing numbers of women are entering occupations that offer higher earnings.
- In June 2013, in a landmark decision, the Supreme Court ruled in favour of 250 female employees of Dumfries and Galloway council who claimed that they were employed under less favourable terms and conditions than certain male employees of the council who did work of equal value.

- In 2001, women accounted for 12.5 per cent of directors on the boards of top companies; today that figure stands at 21 per cent. The Government has set a voluntary target of 25 per cent by 2015. However, Scottish University Ruling Courts are just 25 per cent female, despite female academics making up over 50 per cent of the workforce, and only three of the top 25 posts within Scotland's new single police force were awarded to women.
- In 2013, the Coalition Government announced new tax relief for families where both partners worked. Starting after the 2015 election, the Tax-Free Childcare scheme will cover 20 per cent of working families' childcare costs, up to £6000 per year and per child under 5. It will rise to cover children under 12 in subsequent years. This move is to encourage more women into work: currently 67 per cent of women work compared to 76 per cent of men.

Ethnic minorities

According to the 2011 Census, the black and minority ethnic (BME) population is about 12 per cent of the total UK population. This figure has risen from 3 million in 1991 to almost 7 million today. In Scotland, the minority population is 4 per cent of the total population. The BME community consists of a variety of groups, each of which has different experiences of wealth and poverty. In Scotland, the largest BME groups are Pakistani (30 per cent), Chinese (18 per cent) and Indian (16 per cent). A higher proportion of Bangladeshi, Pakistani and black non-Caribbean groups are living in poverty than any other groups.

Reasons for poverty in the BME communities

Lower income

It is estimated that around two-fifths of people from BME backgrounds live in low-income households – twice the rate of white British people.

Employment

In the past, many migrants had fewer qualifications or qualifications not recognised in the UK, so many were concentrated in low-paid industries such as hotels and catering. The youth unemployment rate for black people has increased at almost twice the rate for white 16- to 24-year-olds since the start of the recession in 2008. Young black men are the worst affected of all.

Culture

Pakistani and Bangladeshi women are mainly Muslim and the cultural expectation is for them to stay at home and look after larger families. Three-quarters of Bangladeshi women and more than two-thirds of Pakistani women are economically inactive.

Poor educational attainment

This explanation has lost its veracity as in the last decade all ethnic groups have improved their average educational attainment. Indian and Bangladeshi students outperform their white counterparts in achieving five A–C passes in GCSE exams. Over 2000 British Pakistanis started a university law course in 2011 compared to 478 in 2001.

Discrimination

Race discrimination in the UK takes three forms: direct discrimination, indirect discrimination and institutional discrimination.

- **Direct discrimination** is when someone is denied an opportunity purely based on their race, ethnic origin, religion or belief.
- **Indirect discrimination** occurs when everyone has to conform to the same practice that would deny a certain group opportunities to practise their religion and celebrate their culture.
- **Institutional discrimination** occurs when an organisation's procedures and policies disadvantage people from ethnic minority backgrounds. It came to the fore in the Macpherson Report into the Metropolitan Police following the Stephen Lawrence Inquiry, where police attitudes to people from BME backgrounds were described as 'institutionally racist'; the police displayed racist stereotyping that disadvantaged minority ethnic people.

Despite earlier legislation such as the Race Relations Act of 1968, discrimination persists. According to an investigation by *The Guardian* in 2012, a significant proportion of people from BME backgrounds believed they had been refused a job because of their race. The Scottish Coalition for Racial Equality and Rights (CRER) claims that people from these backgrounds are much less likely to be appointed to a job within a Scottish local authority than their white counterparts. The CRER's 2014 report indicated that only 0.8 per cent of local government staff are from a BME background – despite making up 4 per cent of the general population of Scotland. Glasgow City Council has the highest number of ethnic minority employees, but this is only 1.9 per cent and according to the 2011 Census the BME population of Glasgow is just under 12 per cent.

Since police began recording racist crimes in 2000 in Scotland, the number of incidents has risen by 75 per cent. Part of this increase may be explained by a greater willingness on the part of victims to report these crimes. However, a report by the Commission for Racial Equality Scotland stated, 'Verbal abuse … was so much a part of everyday life that most people did not think of reporting it.'

A lot of these attacks are concentrated in poorer and disadvantaged areas of cities where many people from BME backgrounds live. Therefore, many who are forced by low income to live in such areas become the target of racist abuse and violence. The perpetrators are mostly youths.

Government responses

- The National Minimum Wage, Working Tax Credit and Child Tax Credit have been used to increase the income of the lowest wage earners in society. As many female and ethnic minority workers suffer from low-income employment, these policies have been of particular benefit to these two groups.

- As women make up a larger proportion of pensioners, Pension Credit has helped improve the income of women who retire with reduced pension entitlement.

- The Equality Act 2010 brings together the previous nine pieces of equality legislation, including legislation covering gender, race and disability. The Act gives women (and men) a right to equal pay for equal work, even if different roles are being carried out. It also says that companies with 250 or more workers have to publish information about the differences in men's and women's pay. The Government plans to do the same for public bodies with 150 or more workers. The Act also allows for positive discrimination: job adverts can be aimed at different ethnic groups or women if the organisation lacks representatives from that particular group. Finally, the Act requires health organisations to eliminate discrimination in the provision of healthcare and thereby reduce health inequalities for BME groups, for example healthcare providers should be aware of the language needs of people living in their areas and provide health promotion in languages other than English.

- The Equality and Human Rights Commission (EHRC) safeguards the human rights of all citizens, especially designated groups. One important role of the EHRC is to monitor and report on pay divisions between the races and genders in unrepresentative public bodies.

- In July 2014, Nicky Morgan was appointed Education Secretary and Minister for Women and Equality. Before 2010, there was no dedicated representation for either group in the Cabinet. This puts equality at the heart of government.

- The Work and Families Act (2006) entitles women to statutory maternity pay (SMP) for 39 weeks and also gives men and women the right to request flexible working hours to care for children under six, disabled children under eighteen and disabled adults. In July 2014, all workers were given the right to request flexible working hours.

Question and model answer

Question ?

Analyse the different lifestyle choices that may result in poor health.

Your may refer to Scotland or to the United Kingdom or both in your answer. **12 marks**

Responses will be credited that make reference to:

- lifestyle choices linked to poor health
- an analysis of the consequences of specific lifestyle choices relating to poor health.

Up to **8 marks** for knowledge (description, explanation and exemplification) and up to **4 marks** for analysis and structured answers.

Remember

Knowledge questions will have either 12 or 20 marks allocated and you will answer one question from a choice of two. If an answer contains more analytical/evaluative points than are required to gain the allocation of 4 marks, these can be credited as knowledge and understanding marks.

Model answer

It is self evident that poor lifestyle choices such as smoking, drinking to excess and poor diet impact on an individual's health. This is the view of those who support the individualist approach which states that an individual's lifestyle choices are responsible for their health. In contrast the collectivist viewpoint is that poverty and social inequality are the driving forces which lead to poor lifestyle choices.

Parts of Scotland are blighted by a 'booze culture' which according to the NHS kills 40 Scots a week. The 2010 Scottish Health Survey indicated that Scots are more likely than drinkers elsewhere in Britain both to binge on alcohol and exceed the recommended daily intake. Daily alcohol consumption in Scotland for both men and women is 25 per cent higher than in England. The terrible impact of this is reflected in official Government statistics. While the alcohol-related deaths per 100,000 of population for the UK is 13 in Shettleston it is 76. This is despite health promotion campaigns to persuade the public to drink in moderation. The SNP Government has passed legislation to introduce alcohol minimum unit pricing but this has been challenged in the courts and has not been implemented.

Obesity is also a lifestyle choice and as a result more and more Scots are becoming obese. It is estimated over 3000 Scots die every year as a direct result of obesity

Again despite anti-smoking campaigns and the ban on smoking in public places too many Scots still smoke. The consequences of smoking can be fatal – every year there are more than 13,000 smoking-related deaths in Scotland alone. There is a clear link between smoking and lung cancer and Scots are more likely to smoke than their English counterparts. Medical evidence indicates that lung cancer rates are 49 per cent higher in Scotland than in England and Wales.

However, it is clear that obesity and smoking and alcohol abuse are social class and poverty issues. While the number of women in Social class 1 who are obese is about 13%, the figure for Social class v is over 25%. Obesity is linked to heart disease, diabetes and premature death. The figures for smoking also display the wealth/poverty divide. While 44% of people in Nitshill (a deprived area of Glasgow) smoke, only 15% in Clarkston (wealthy area) smoke.

The SNP Government's Equally well report on health inequalities concludes 'that there is a clear relationship between income inequality and health inequality'. It states that more than 2/3 of the total alcohol-related deaths were in the most deprived areas and that those living in the most deprived areas of Scotland have a suicide risk double that of the Scottish average. It is difficult to make lifestyle choices when you are unemployed living in poor housing and in a deprived area. Membership of a gym, private health care, health foods and a jog in the park belong to a different world.

Marker's comment

This is an excellent answer because it is rich in knowledge and analysis. Each point is fully developed with relevant up-to-date description and explanation. The impact of obesity and especially of alcohol and smoking are fully developed and, impressively, are also linked to poverty and social inequality. This answer would gain full marks. **12/12**

Chapter 7

Crime and the law

> ## What you should know 👍
>
> To be successful in this section, you should know about:
> - ★ the role of law in society: the Scottish legal system
> - ★ theories and causes of crime
> - ★ the impact of crime on society
> - ★ methods of tackling crime and their effectiveness: police and recent legislation
> - ★ methods of tackling crime and their effectiveness: the penal system.

The Scottish criminal justice system

Scotland retained its own legal system after the Act of Union in 1707 and Scots law is still the system we use today. Most law and order issues have been devolved to the Scottish Parliament (terrorism is one of the exceptions) and new laws are continually being passed or considered. The Scottish Government, for example, lowered the drink-driving limit in December 2014.

The Crown Office and Procurator Fiscal Service

In Scotland it is the Crown Office and Procurator Fiscal Office (COPFS) that decides whether or not to charge and prosecute individuals. It is responsible for prosecuting criminals and investigating complaints against the police. In an average year, it handles almost 300,000 reports of offences. The COPFS is headed by the Lord Advocate who, alongside the Solicitor General, is the principal legal adviser to the Scottish Government. The most serious High Court prosecutions are conducted by the Lord Advocate himself. For other cases at the High Court, experienced solicitors called advocates depute carry out prosecutions.

How does the court system work in Scotland?

There are three types of court in Scotland that deal with different levels of offending:
- the High Court of Justiciary
- the Sheriff Courts
- Justice of the Peace Courts.

The High Court of Justiciary

The High Court is the supreme criminal court in Scotland and deals with the most serious of crimes. The High Court is presided over by the Lord Justice General and the Lord Justice Clerk and has a jury of fifteen members of the public. The custodial sentencing powers of the High Court are unlimited. When dealing with crimes such as murder, statute dictates that life imprisonment is imposed. The High Court also deals with all criminal appeal cases. For all appeals, at least two judges will preside but this may increase to five in complex cases.

The Sheriff Courts

A sheriff, who is an experienced solicitor or advocate, presides over trials at a Sheriff Court. Most criminal and civil cases in Scotland are dealt with in a Sheriff Court. In **solemn criminal hearing procedures** a jury sits, while in **summary criminal hearing procedures** the sheriff decides whether the accused is innocent or guilty, and, if the latter, they will also decide on the appropriate sentence.

- For solemn cases, the maximum sentence available to a sheriff is five years' imprisonment and/or an unlimited fine.
- For summary cases, twelve months' imprisonment and/or a fine of up to £5000 is available.
- A guilty verdict can be referred to the High Court of the Justiciary for sentencing if the sheriff decides that the crime merits a more severe sentence.

Justice of the Peace Courts

A Justice of the Peace Court is a lay court where the Justice of the Peace (JP) is supported by a legally qualified clerk. The Court deals with less serious cases, such as theft, drunk and disorderly and traffic offences. The maximum sentence that a JP may impose is 60 days' imprisonment or a fine not exceeding £2500. In Glasgow's JP Courts, legally qualified 'stipendiary magistrates' have the same powers as in Sheriff Courts.

Court of Session

The Court of Session is Scotland's supreme civil court and sits in Edinburgh. It is both a trial court and a court of appeal. Although most civil cases take place at Sheriff Court level, high-profile cases involving large companies or sizable sums of money are heard at the Court of Session, for example much of the legal wrangling centring on Rangers Football Club has been heard at the Court of Session.

UK Supreme Court

The creation of the UK Supreme Court in 2009 has led to accusations that it is undermining the independence and distinctiveness of the Scottish legal system. The Supreme Court is regarded as the UK's highest court and argues that it can judge Scottish appeals if the accused is appealing under European Court of Human Rights (ECHR) legislation, for example in 2011, Nat Fraser, who had been found guilty of murdering his wife in 2003, appealed to the UK Supreme Court. Its verdict was that he should be retried in the High Court in Edinburgh and in 2012 he was found guilty for a second time.

Key words

Solemn criminal hearing procedures: Trials such as murder, rape or serious assault are conducted in the High Court of Justiciary or Sheriff Court with a judge and a jury. In Scotland, a jury of fifteen decides on the verdict of cases and a simple majority is needed to determine the outcome of the verdict.

Summary criminal hearing procedures: Offences such as breach of the peace are heard in a Sheriff Court or a Justice of the Peace Court without a jury.

A June 2014 decision by the UK Supreme Court had serious implications for Scotland. The Court ruled that a trial of suspected terrorists could be held in total secrecy on grounds of national security. This decision goes against the basic principle that justice must be seen to be done and undermines citizens' rights. If a similar trial were held in Scotland and Scottish judges refused to hold it in secret, the UK Government could appeal to the Supreme Court.

Verdicts in Scottish courts

There are three verdicts that a jury can arrive at in Scottish criminal courts:

Guilty

A 'guilty' verdict can lead to a wide range of sentencing options, such as prison or community service.

Not guilty

A 'not guilty' verdict means that the accused is found innocent and, until recently, could not be prosecuted again on that charge. However, following changes in England, a new **double jeopardy** (Scotland) Act 2011 allows a second trial if compelling new evidence emerges.

Not proven

A 'not proven' verdict is unique to Scotland. The accused is free to go but with the implication that they have escaped conviction *only* because of some doubt or lack of evidence. In 2012, MSP Michael McMahon launched a consultation into this verdict as he believes it is 'illogical, inconsistent and confusing'.

It is argued that jurors are confused by this verdict, and the high profile trial of John Wilson in 2011 seems to support this view. The jury of eight men and seven women decided that the charge against him of assaulting Neil Lennon, then Celtic FC manager, merited a verdict of 'not proven'. This was despite the accused's admission that he had, during the Hearts–Celtic match in May 2011, run at the Celtic dug-out, swore and lunged at Neil Lennon, and struck him on the head. The incident had occurred at a televised match and so clear evidence of his guilt was available. He was found guilty of a lesser charge.

> ### Key word
>
> **Double jeopardy:**
> The legal principle that prevents people being tried for the same crime twice.

The Children's Hearings System

The Children's Hearings System is the care and justice system for Scotland's children and young people. A fundamental principle is that children who commit offences, and children who need care and protection, are dealt with in the same system – as these are often the same children.

At the heart of the system are Children's Reporters, who are based in local communities. Children and young people are referred to the Reporter from a number of sources, including police, social work, education and health. They are referred because some aspect of their life is giving cause for concern.

The Reporter investigates each referral and determines whether compulsory measures of intervention are required; if they are, a Children's Hearing will be held.

The Hearing consists of three panel members, who are all trained volunteers from the local community. The Hearing listens to the child's circumstances and then decides what measures are required. The child may need a particular type of treatment or intervention, or they may be placed with foster carers, or in a residential unit or secure accommodation. The Hearing may decide that the child should remain at home with support from other agencies, such as social work.

The Hearings System aims to ensure that the best interests of the child are met and that they receive the most appropriate intervention and support.

The Scottish Children's Reporter Administration (SCRA) is one of the agencies that has a responsibility for how the Children's Hearings System operates. Focused on children and young people most at risk, SCRA's role and purpose is to:

SCOTTISH
CHILDREN'S REPORTER
ADMINISTRATION

Figure 7.1 The Scottish Children's Reporter Administration logo

- make effective decisions about a need to refer a child to a Children's Hearing
- enable children and families to participate in Hearings
- provide suitable accommodation and facilities for Hearings.

Further information about SCRA can be found at www.scra.gov.uk.

Another of these agencies is Children's Hearings Scotland (CHS), a relatively new public body established by the Children's Hearings (Scotland) Act 2011. The Act created the role of National Convener, to act as a voice for Scotland's 2500 volunteer panel members and to ensure they are consistently supported to a high standard. The Act created CHS as a dedicated national body, to support the National Convener in the delivery of functions related to the recruitment, selection, appointment, training, retention and support of panel members. Further information about CHS and the Children's Hearings system can be found at www.chscotland.gov.uk.

children's
**hearings
scotland**

Figure 7.2 The Children's Hearings Scotland logo

Key facts

A total of 19,077 children were referred to the Reporter in 2013–14, which represents 2.1 per cent of all children in Scotland. Referrals are split into two broad categories:

- care and protection: where the welfare of the child is causing concern
- offence: where the child is believed to have committed an offence.

The majority of children are referred on care and protection grounds. The most common grounds of referral in 2013–14 were 'lack of parental care', which includes 'close connection with a person who has carried out domestic abuse' and 'victim of a Schedule 1 offence'. The number of children referred on offence grounds has decreased for the seventh consecutive year. The most common types of alleged offences are assault, vandalism and threatening or abusive behaviour. Eight years old is the criminal age of responsibility in Scotland – children aged under eight cannot be referred to the Reporter for offending.

Compulsory Supervision Orders (CSOs) are the most common form of compulsory intervention made by Hearings as they are the only longer-term option available.

- 4664 children aged under eight were subject to CSOs in 2013–14.
- Among all children under 16 there were 11,420 CSOs. The age at which children can be charged is twelve.

Child protection

Hearings can make short-term decisions to address emergency and/or high-risk situations where measures have to be put in place immediately to protect children or address their behaviour. This may include Hearings arranged as a result of the sheriff granting a Child Protection Order (CPO). The granting of a CPO requires the child to be removed to (or kept in) a place of safety away from home. For this measure to be considered, a child must be at risk of significant harm.

More CPOs are granted for very young children, reflecting their greater vulnerability and requirement for immediate protection. Hearings can also make an Interim Compulsory Supervision Order if they are unable to make a final decision but have concerns about a child. It might say where the child must live or other conditions that must be followed.

Source: Scottish Children's Reporter Administration

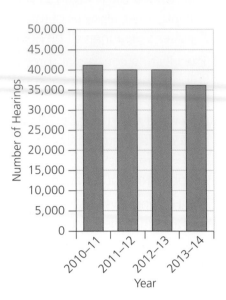
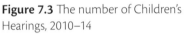

Figure 7.3 The number of Children's Hearings, 2010–14

Theories and causes of crime

Criminologists and sociologists have long considered the factors that lead to crime. They ask themselves whether some individuals are born evil (nature) or whether it is the environment they grow up in that makes them carry out criminal acts (nurture). This is referred to as the nature/nurture debate. Criminology is the scientific study of the nature, extent, causes and control of criminal behaviour in both the individual and in society. Two main theories of crime are:

- biological and psychological
- sociological.

Biological and physiological theories

This theory of crime was very popular in the late nineteenth and early twentieth centuries. Criminologists such as Cesare Lombroso claimed to be able to identify criminals from bodily characteristics, such as high cheek bones, fat lips and large ears. Later supporters of the biological school highlighted aspects of intelligence, personality traits and chromosomes. Twins and adoption studies give some support to the view that genetics have important influences on criminal behaviour.

Evidence suggests a link between imprisonment and those with conditions such as ADHD and depression. A young person struggling to control their ADHD may fail first at home, then at school, next at work and then finally with the law.

Hans Eysenck, a British psychologist, claimed that psychological factors such as extraversion and neuroticism made a person more likely to commit criminal acts.

The popular press tends to label those who commit violent murders as 'evil'. One such example was the murder of toddler James Bulger in 1993 in Merseyside. Two ten-year-old boys, Robert Thompson and Jon Venables, were charged and found guilty of murder. According to the tabloid press they were 'sons of Satan'; however, their family backgrounds displayed classic risk factors, including a chaotic lifestyle, poverty, alcoholism, marital breakdown, neglect and bullying.

Sociological theories

The sociological theory states that the individual is shaped by their experiences within family, community and friendship groups and by their socio-economic status. As such, it is a complex combination of factors that leads people to commit crimes, for example the vast majority of people who suffer poverty will never commit a crime. However, for a young person, the influence of sustained poverty combined with poor upbringing and peer pressure may lead them down a path of offending.

Sociological theories of crime

Chicago School

Chicago School sociologists highlight the importance of the urban neighbourhood in explaining crime. Urban areas with high levels of deprivation often experience breakdown in the social structure and institutions such as family and school. This creates an environment ripe for deviant behaviour, which leads to hotspots of crime.

Strain Theory

American sociologist Robert Merton highlighted that most mainstream cultures, especially in the USA, are centred around the dreams of opportunity, prosperity and freedom. This 'American Dream' becomes an intoxicating cultural and psychological motivation. However, if the social structure of opportunities is unequal and leads to many in society being denied the dream, some will turn to crime to achieve or maintain wealth and status. Others drop into deviant subcultures such as gangs and urban homelessness.

The causes of crime

Economic factors/poverty

Although there is no direct link between poverty and crime, evidence would suggest that those who are poor may be tempted to commit crime. Those who experience social exclusion are more likely to suffer from alcohol/drug addition, poor mental health and homelessness. There is a clear link between social exclusion and crime.

Youth crime

In 2013, according to the Scottish Government, 43 per cent of all crimes and offences in Scotland were attributable to young people under the age of 21. Young people are responsible for higher proportions of offences such as fire-raising (86 per cent of offences are committed by young people), vandalism (75 per cent), theft of motor vehicles (75 per cent), handling offensive weapons (59 per cent) and housebreaking (55 per cent). The media tend to demonise young people with comments such as 'feral youths stalking our streets'.

Young people are also associated with gang culture and the influence of peer pressure. Recent studies have found that up to 3500 young people between the ages of 11 and 23 have joined one of the 170 street gangs within Glasgow's borders. Gangs can be felt to offer protection, status, conformity, a sense of community and excitement.

Level of education

There is a link between poor educational attainment and committing crime. Those who leave school as a NEET (Not in Education, Employment or Training) find it difficult to go on and gain employment. Children who are excluded from school are at risk of drifting into a life of crime.

Alcohol and drugs

Alcohol abuse is linked to many crimes, especially violent crimes. Nearly half of all of Scotland's prisoners say that they were under the influence of alcohol at the time of their offence. According to a report by *The Herald*, academics at Glasgow University have found that people living in an area with six alcohol outlets or more can expect crime rates twice as high as those in an area with only three.

Drugs account for 29 per cent of violent crimes. Drug abusers are more likely to commit crimes such as burglary and muggings to fund their habit. However, it is debatable whether drugs actually lead people to commit crimes or whether those who use drugs are predisposed to a life of crime.

Greed and white-collar crime

Individuals who engage in corruption to finance an extravagant lifestyle can be motivated by greed. One recent example was Jurgen Whitehouse, an IT services boss at Ofcom who was sentenced to two and a half years in prison for defrauding the telecoms regulator out of more than £500,000. The problem with **white-collar crime** is that as it is non-violent, not obvious and rarely committed against one victim it is very hard to detect and prove.

> ### Key word
>
> **White-collar crime:** When fraud, embezzlement or other illegal schemes are used, mainly in the financial sector.

The impact of crime on society

Crime can have a terrible impact on individuals and their community, placing many in a state of fear (as illustrated in the anti-rape march described over the page). There are also financial costs to crime: the criminal justice system is not cheap, and there are costs associated with police services, court services and punishments.

Groups most likely to be victims of crime

Those living in poverty

Those who live in poorer areas are twice as likely to be a victim of crime and are also most likely to be repeat victims.

Young people

Young people are more likely to be victims of violent crimes, such as muggings and assault. According to the Scottish Crime and Justice Survey 2013, 8.2 per cent of those aged 16 to 24 reported being victims of violent crime; the figure is only 1.9 per cent among those aged 45 to 59.

Elderly people

The charity Age UK found that almost half of people aged over 75 are too afraid to leave their homes after dark because they believe they would be subject to verbal abuse or muggings. In recent years, criminal gangs have targeted elderly people to attempt to trap them in financial scams.

Women

According to pressure group the Fawcett Society, at least one woman in four experiences domestic violence in her lifetime, and between one in eight and one in ten experiences it annually.

More than 5000 join anti-rape midnight protest

More than 5000 people have taken part in a peaceful protest in Glasgow's South Side, which circled around the area where a 24-year-old woman was raped in May 2014. The walk came about following four sexual assaults in the city in as many weeks.

Two Govanhill residents, Ashley Crossan and Amanda Johnston, organised These Streets Were Made For Walking as a 'show of solidarity in support of the victims of rape and a call to action'.

Adapted from an article by Martin Williams from *The Herald*, 10 June 2014

Figure 7.4 The group marching in protest

The impact of crime on the offender

Committing a crime and receiving a prison sentence can have huge personal consequences for offenders and their families. Once released, many convicted criminals find life extremely difficult:

- They may suffer unemployment or difficulty in finding work because of their criminal record.
- They could be homeless, having lost their homes while in prison.
- They may experience marital difficulties created by the stress of being away from their spouses, and perhaps by the separation from their children.
- Some families can experience a great deal of shame and embarrassment, be the target of bullying or revenge attacks and even be forced out of communities altogether.

The impact of crime on the community

High levels of crime may damage community spirit and result in less neighbourliness. It leads people to prefer to 'keep themselves to themselves' out of fear of harassment or becoming involved in arguments that may lead to a criminal act. Areas with high levels of crime often suffer from vandalism and graffiti, making them less desirable and potentially more dangerous.

Some crimes can rally a community together, as illustrated by the June 2014 anti-rape march in Glasgow (see above). A further example was in Blantyre in 2011, when thousands of people from communities around Blantyre marched against the use of knives and in support of murdered teenager Reamonn Gormley's family.

The economic impact of crime

Theft, such as shoplifting, costs businesses: *The Guardian* reported in January 2013 that retail crime is estimated to cost the sector over £1.6 billion per year. Violent crime costs the UK economy more than £124 billion a year, equivalent to £4700 for every household, and identity theft costs the UK over £2.7 billion. According to the Scottish Government, over £2.5 billion was budgeted for criminal justice in 2013–14.

The political impact of crime

Public and media pressure can persuade the government to bring in new laws such as:

Sarah's Law

In 2000, an eight-year-old girl, Sarah Payne, was abducted and murdered by Roy Whiting, who had previously been convicted of abducting and indecently assaulting a young girl. The *News of the World* newspaper led a nationwide campaign for better protection. New laws in England and Scotland were set up so that parents and carers can request criminal records held by police for people who have access to children.

Clare's Law

Following the murder of Clare Wood by her ex-partner, it was disclosed that he had a disturbing history of savage violence towards women. Her family and the media campaigned for greater disclosure, and in 2014 a new law in England and Wales allowed the police to disclose information on request about a partner's previous history of domestic violence or violent acts. The Scottish Government is considering its introduction.

The 2011 English riots

The Government's failure to prevent and control the 2011 riots that took place in London, Manchester, Birmingham, Bristol and Liverpool led to strong action being taken against the rioters. Five people died and 2500 shops and businesses were damaged or destroyed. One judge explained that such criminal behaviour 'must be met with sentences longer than they would be if the offences had been committed in isolation'. Those involved in the riots received sentences of up to two or three times longer than the normal term.

The role of the police in tackling crime

The main roles of the police are to:

- protect the public
- ensure law and order is maintained in society
- detect criminals
- prevent crime.

Police Scotland

- Police Scotland came into being in April 2013.
- It is the second largest force in the UK after the Metropolitan Police.
- It is a merger of the eight Scottish police forces and includes the Scottish Police College and the Scottish Crime and Drug Enforcement Agency.
- There are fourteen local policing divisions, each headed by a Local Police Commander who ensures that local policing in each area is responsive, accountable and tailored to meet local needs.

- The Police Scotland budget in 2013–14 was £1.1 billion, although budget cuts are required over the next few years.
- Police Scotland is led by Chief Constable Sir Stephen House, the former chief constable of Strathclyde Police.
- There are 17,234 police officers in Scotland and 6701 police support staff.
  Source: www.scotland.police.uk

Crime prevention

Preventing crime before it happens is an example of effective policing. The Violence Reduction Unit (VRU) helps to reduce violent crime in Scotland. In 2010, the VRU achieved success with a community initiative to reduce violence in Glasgow's East End, cutting gang crime by over 50 per cent and engaging many youths who felt isolated from society and caught up in gang culture.

Knife-crime prevention

In 2012, the Scottish Government increased the maximum sentence for those found carrying a knife from four years to five. Campaigns such as *No Knives, Better Lives* educate young people about the dangers of carrying a knife and the devastating personal consequences it can have on their future.

Wide use of stop and search by police discourages young people from carrying knives. However, this policy has been criticised. In June 2014, Police Scotland stated that routine stop and searches of young people would now end. During the first nine months of the existence of the new single force, 223 searches were undertaken on children aged nine or under. A Liberal Democrat MSP (Alison McInnes) stated that the end of routine searches was a 'victory for children and their rights'.

Crimes of handling an offensive weapon have fallen dramatically in Scotland, by 67 per cent in Glasgow and 60 per cent in Scotland since 2006–07, according to the *Daily Record*.

Community policing

Working with the community reflects the view that policing is a partnership with local citizens. This should help the public to feel safer and to have greater confidence in the police and lead to a drop in crime. However, the revelation in 2014 that police regularly carry handguns while on patrol has been criticised by some MSPs. They argue that this weakens community policing and is a step towards the militarisation of the police.

The penal system

Figure 7.5 highlights that the action taken against those who commit crimes is not simply to punish but to deter and rehabilitate the criminal, thus reducing reoffending in the future. Many now question the effectiveness of a prison sentence for less serious crime and argue that alternatives to prison are more effective.

Figure 7.5 The purpose of imprisonment

Prisons work

- At any one time, over 90,000 UK criminals are locked up, thereby protecting the public.
- The victims of crime feel that justice has been done. The criminal is denied liberty and separated from family and friends.
- The possibility of a prison sentence deters individuals from committing crime.
- Prisons offer prisoners opportunities to receive treatment if they have drug or mental health issues.
- For violent crimes including murder, society must protect its citizens by imposing custodial sentences.

Prisons fail

- Many criminals go in and out of jail, never being deterred or reformed, but only ever being further criminalised: 75 per cent of short-term prisoners reoffend.
- Overcrowding in prisons limits the number of prisoners who can take part in educational and offending behaviour programmes; there is insufficient space on these programmes for all prisoners.
- Overcrowding can create violent and chaotic conditions and makes it difficult for prison officers to control abuse of drugs and acts of violence between prisoners.
- Around 70 per cent of prisoners have histories of poor mental health and/or drug problems. In total, 28 prisoners have committed suicide between 2010 and 2013 and 61 have attempted suicide.

Source: www.gov.uk

Scottish female prisoner statistics

- The proportion of female prisoners in Scotland has increased from 3.5 per cent of the prison population in 2000 to 5.7 per cent in 2012.
- 80 per cent of women in Cornton Vale Prison have mental health issues.
- Female prisoners are ten times more likely to self-harm than male prisoners.
- 71 per cent of women in Cornton Vale have used drugs before being sent to prison.
- 71 per cent of women in prison have no qualifications. This compares to 15 per cent of the general population.
- Since 2008, 32 babies have been born while their mother was in Cornton Vale.
- Some 16,500 children each year in Scotland are directly affected by parental imprisonment. Fifty per cent of children in care go on to receive custodial sentences.
- The Elish Angiolini Commission into the treatment of female prisoners called for fewer women to be sent to prison: 75 per cent of female prisoners receive sentences of six months or less and the reoffending rate of these short-term prisoners is 80 per cent.

Prison statistics

- In 2009 the number of Scottish prisoners passed 8000 for the first time.
- In January 2014, two Scottish Victorian prisons – HMP Peterhead and HMP Aberdeen – were closed. A new super-jail – HMP Grampian – opened in 2014.
- The total number of prisoners in England and Wales is 85,500 and in Scotland it is just under 8300.

Source: www.sps.gov.uk

Alternatives to prison

In January 2014, Lord Carloway, one of Scotland's most senior judges, argued that the penal system should concentrate more on rehabilitation and less on retribution, and that this would be in the interests of society. The use of fines, community payback orders and home-detention curfews are alternatives to prison sentences.

Arguments for and against alternatives to prison

Arguments for

- Sending a criminal to prison for a year costs a minimum of £30,000; tagging an offender costs about £2000. The average cost of a community payback order is around £2400, which is approximately half the cost of a two-month prison sentence.
- Alternatives to prison allow offenders to remain with their families and may prevent family break-up and children being put into care.
- The offender can make restitution for their crime by improving the community.
- Offenders avoid the stigma of imprisonment and the possibility of falling into bad company and criminal culture in prison.
- The reoffending rate is lower for offenders who receive a non-custodial sentence compared to those who are imprisoned.

Arguments against

- The public and media perception is that alternatives to prison are soft options and fail to punish the prisoner. Many victims feel that the offender has received nothing more than 'a slap on the wrist'.
- Enforcement and monitoring offenders can be a problem: In May 2014, figures were released that showed that more than one-third of penalties issued as an alternative to prosecution had not been paid. Outstanding payments going back to 2010 stand at £5 million. Many offenders fail to complete their community service.
- Many offenders break home-detention curfews and commit crimes. The private companies that monitor curfews overcharge for the services they provide.
- It is time consuming and costly to take offenders before the courts for failure to comply with crime prevention orders.

Main alternatives to prison

Electronic monitoring or tagging

Electronic monitoring or tagging has been used to enforce the home-detention curfew since its introduction in 2006. The service is run by the private sector. SERCO, the private company that runs the service in England and Wales, overcharged the UK government by over £20 million. In Scotland, the security service is provided by G4S and the contract in Scotland is worth £13 million over five years.

Community orders

A court can order between 80 and 300 hours of supervised work, which must be completed within six months of the date of sentence. The offender can carry out their sentence in their free time if they are in full- or part-time work. They are also encouraged to tackle any addiction issues: in 2010, over 1700 UK offenders were placed on community sentence orders that involved drug treatment.

Disposal order fines

The two main types of financial penalty are fines and compensation. This combines elements of:

- **retribution** – based on the seriousness of the crime
- **deterrence** – showing the offender that crime does not pay
- **reparation** – paying the victim or society back for harm done.

Question and model answer

Question ?

Analyse the impact of crime on different groups in society.

You should refer to Scotland or to the United Kingdom or both in your answer. **12 marks**

Responses will be credited that make reference to:

- ○ a range of different crimes and/or those most vulnerable to crime
- ○ an analysis of the impact of crime on different groups.

Up to **8 marks** for knowledge (description, explanation and exemplification) and up to **4 marks** for analysis and structured answers.

Remember

Knowledge questions will have either 12 or 20 marks allocated and you will answer one question from a choice of two. If an answer contains more analytical/evaluative points than are required to gain the allocation of 4 marks, these can be credited as knowledge and understanding marks.

Model answer

Groups most likely to be victims of crime are the young and those who live in poverty. However the elderly tend to suffer the most even though they are less likely to be victims of crime. The impact of crime on these groups can be devastating.

According to the 2013 SCJS over 8 per cent of those aged 16–24 reported being victims of violent crime compared to less than 2 per cent for those aged 45–49. Young people are also more likely to be assaulted without injury followed by personal theft – mostly mobile phones. The consequence is that some young people do not feel safe and may carry a knife which can lead to arrest by the police. In extreme cases young people can be murdered as happened in 2011 to Reamon Gormley in Blantyre. As such it is also the families that suffer and also the community. The people of Blantyre marched through the streets to honour Reamonn and to demand action against knife crime.

1 in 5 of those who live in deprived areas are victims of reported crime, including assault and burglary. Given that many people especially in deprived areas do not report crime the real figure is much higher. The consequences of burglary impact emotionally and financially on the individual and community. Individuals do not feel safe in their own home and can lose valuable possessions. Again in these areas home insurance will be higher and in fact many victims cannot afford home insurance with premiums so high. So they will not be able to replace the stolen goods. Again these deprived communities with high violent crime rates can experience poor health brought on by stress and fear. In 2010 it was reported that 42 per cent of residents in Springburn feared being attacked in their neighbourhood compared to 10 per cent in affluent areas.

For the elderly to experience crime can devastate their life. A mugging can damage their frail bodies and take away their ability to lead an independent life. The charity Age UK found that about 50% of those aged over 75 are too afraid to leave their homes after dark. The impact for the elderly can be isolation, depression and anxiety.

Marker's comment

This is an excellent answer because it is rich in *knowledge* and *analysis*. Each point is fully developed with relevant up-to-date description and explanation. The candidate identifies young, poor and elderly people as key victims (three developed points). The consequences for the victims of violent crime and theft are fully developed, with reference to up-to-date crime statistics and exemplification. This answer would gain full marks.   **12/12**

Part Four: International issues

This section of the book provides summary course notes for the International Issues unit of the course.

You will have studied one of the following topics as part of your CfE Higher International Issues unit:

- World Powers
- World Issues.

World Powers refer to members of the G20 organisation that represent more than 85 per cent of the world's economies. In this revision book, we will concentrate on the USA, China and South Africa.

In the World Issues section of the International Issues unit we will concentrate on the causes, consequences and attempts at resolution of a particular world issue; in this case, development issues in Africa.

In the extended response/essay section of the exam you will answer either a 12-mark question or a 20-mark question.

Chapter 8

World powers: The United States of America

What you should know 👍

SQA requirements

To be successful in this section, you should know about:

★ the USA: its political system and process:
  - ★ constitutional arrangements and the main institutions of government
  - ★ the political rights and responsibilities of citizens
  - ★ influencing the political process and opportunities for participation
  - ★ evaluating the political system and the extent of democratic influence and control
★ the USA: recent socio-economic issues:
  - ★ the nature and extent of socio-economic issues
  - ★ government responses to socio-economic issues
  - ★ the effectiveness of government responses to socio-economic issues
★ the role of the USA in international relations:
  - ★ involvement in international organisations
  - ★ relationship with other countries
  - ★ evaluating international influence and power.

Introduction

The USA is the third largest country in the world (by area) and has a very diverse population of 316 million people. The main ethnic group in the USA is white, but there are also large populations of black Americans, Hispanic Americans and Asian or Pacific Islanders (APIs).

The USA's government is split on three main levels: local county, state and federal (national) level. Each of the 50 states has the power to make decisions on state matters and the Federal Government oversees all national laws and policies.

People

There are several main ethnic groups in the USA. Because of its long-standing reputation as the 'land of opportunity', many people have moved to the USA over the years to settle. The main ethnic groups are:

- **white**, who make up around 63 per cent of the population and are the dominant ethnic group
- **black/African American**, who make up around 13 per cent of the population and mainly live in the South

- **Hispanic/Latino**, who make up around 17 per cent of the population and tend to come from areas such as Mexico, Cuba and Puerto Rico – both legally and illegally
- **Asian**, who make up around 5 per cent of the population and mostly come from China, Korea and Japan, which are closer to the west coast of America
- **Native American**, who now only make up around 1 per cent of the population; they are the indigenous population of the USA.

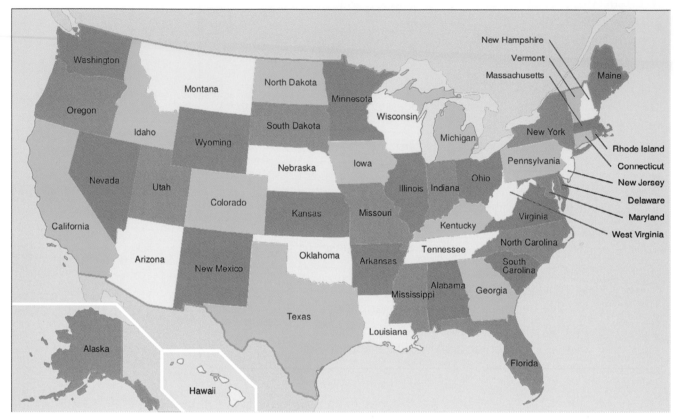

Figure 8.1 The USA

The US political system

The USA was founded back in the 1780s, when the country gained its independence and the Constitution of the USA was written. This written Constitution outlines the US government's powers, its structure and the role of each of the three branches of the US government: the Legislative, Executive and Judicial. The first ten amendments of the Constitution make up the Bill of Rights, which outlines the rights of all American citizens.

Rights and responsibilities

Rights	Responsibilities
To vote	To participate in politics and choose the leaders
To run for office	To respect the views of other people and of other political parties
To free speech	To respect other opinions that differ from your own

Table 8.1 Some of the rights and responsibilities of American citizens

Federal Government

The Federal Government is made up of three main branches whose roles are outlined in the Constitution. The system is based on the **separation of powers**; the idea that in a democracy no one branch can have ultimate control or power to make decisions by themselves. This provides **checks and balances** on the US political system to ensure that actions carried out by the Federal Government are agreed by all three branches.

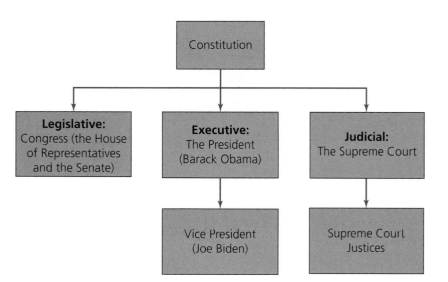

Figure 8.2 The National/Federal Government

Three branches

Legislative

Congress (the House of Representatives and the Senate) is responsible for making the laws or passing legislation. The Senate currently has 100 Senators – two for each state. There are also 435 Representatives in the House of Representatives, and the number of Representatives from each state is based on the size of the state's population. The composition of Congress changes every two years with the mid-term elections, which cover all of the House of Representatives and one-third of the Senate.

Executive

The president, vice president and cabinet are responsible for creating government policies. The president is also head of state.

Judicial

This branch is responsible for ensuring that all new laws to be passed by Congress, and actions to be made by the president, are constitutional. The president appoints judges to serve on the Supreme Court when a vacancy arises. The Court's role is extremely important: it ensures that the rights of Americans enshrined in the Constitution are protected.

Powers of the president

Many people regard the president of the United States as one of the most powerful people in the world. However, the USA is a democracy and although Barack Obama has many important powers as president, there

Key words

Separation of powers: To ensure the American political system is as democratic as possible, the Constitution outlines how powers are separated between Congress, President and the Supreme Court so that co-operation is needed between them before action can be taken.

Checks and balances: The three branches of the Federal Government (Congress, President and the Supreme Court) all have the power to check each other: they can prevent one of the other branches from becoming too powerful by stopping them from taking a particular action. This means that power is balanced between the three branches because they have to agree with what the other branches are doing.

are also many important limits to his power. The three branches structure outlined on the previous page ensures that the president can never have ultimate control, and his actions are checked by both the Supreme Court and Congress. However, the president still has the power to:

- **suggest new policies:** he can suggest new policies that the government wants to put forward, for example the Affordable Care Act ('Obamacare'); this is usually done at the president's annual State of the Union Address to Congress and the American people
- **veto laws:** the use of the president's veto means that he can block or reject any law put forward by Congress to prevent it from being passed, for example Obama has vetoed two laws so far in his presidency, meaning that they have not been passed; Congress can overturn the veto if two-thirds of Congress reject it, and this usually happens when the Senate and the House of Representatives are controlled by a hostile party
- **act as the US figurehead:** the president is responsible for appointing ambassadors and making treaties with other countries; he is also head of state
- **command the armed forces:** the president is commander-in-chief (head) of the armed forces and can therefore order and mobilise troops, for example Obama sent troops to kill Osama Bin Laden in 2011
- **appoint justices:** the president has the power to appoint judges to the Supreme Court, for example in 2009 Obama appointed the first Hispanic and third female Justice, Sonia Sotomayor; however, his nominee must be approved by the Senate
- **appoint his own cabinet:** the president has powers of patronage, for example John Kerry is Obama's Secretary of State.

Limits on the powers of the president

The Supreme Court and Congress check the powers of the president to ensure that they cannot become too powerful:

The Supreme Court limits the president's powers by:

- **deeming laws unconstitutional:** the Supreme Court can decide to reject any law if they believe it goes against the Constitution of the USA or the Bill of Rights; parts of Obama's Affordable Care Act ('Obamacare') were initially rejected because they were unconstitutional and the bill had to be redrafted.

Congress limits the powers of the president by:

- **retaining the right to declare war:** only Congress can declare war on another country, even though the president is commander-in-chief of the armed forces
- **preventing presidential policies from progressing:** Congress can block any policies put forward by the president, and also decide the funds put towards each presidential policy; therefore, Congress can affect the success of presidential policies

- **overturning the president's veto:** although the president has the power to veto (reject) laws passed by Congress, Congress can overturn his veto with a two-thirds majority vote and the law will pass
- **impeaching the president:** this means that Congress can get rid of the president, again only with a two-thirds majority vote and by following the legal process; the real risk of this is very low – there have been only two attempts to impeach a president over the last 80 years: President Nixon and President Clinton.

Other factors limiting the president's powers

The president is limited in the time they can serve as president; they can only serve a maximum of two four-year terms in office. This means that towards the end of a term, the president may struggle to implement policies and get backing for their proposals from Congress.

The composition of Congress can limit the president's power. Currently, the House of Representatives and Senate (from January 2015) are controlled by the **Republicans**, who are hostile to the President. This can lead to gridlock and weak government. In 2013, the President's proposal for tighter gun controls following a mass shooting in Sandy Hook failed due to a lack of support from the Republican Party in Congress. In October 2013, the Federal Government faced a financial crisis: The Republicans refused to accept the budget unless changes were made to the Affordable Care Act. Obama refused to back down; eventually a deal was agreed and the budget was passed, but this stalemate damaged the US economy.

Presidential Election 2012

Barack Obama was re-elected President in 2012 after defeating Republican candidate Mitt Romney. His running mate and Vice President is Joe Biden. Obama has proven popular with voters for many reasons, which are hard to pin down; these include that he is young compared to his predecessors, that he is the first black president and that the **Democrats'** collectivist policies often appeal more to voters during a time of recession and hardship.

Voting patterns and participation in politics

Ways of participating in politics

The American people can participate in politics in very similar ways to the British public. They can:
- stand for office
- join a political party (Democrats or Republicans or its pressure group the Tea Party)
- campaign for presidential candidates, senators or governors
- join interest groups
- vote during local, state and national elections.

Key words

Republicans:
A political party associated with Presidents such as George W. Bush and candidates such as Mitt Romney and Jeb Bush. The Republicans tend to have more right-wing, individualist policies that reflect the ideas of capitalism and gun ownership.

Democrats:
A political party associated with Presidents such as Obama. The Democrats tend to have more left-wing, collectivist policies that often benefit ethnic-minority groups and women.

Voting patterns in the USA

Voters are influenced on who they vote for by different factors, including income, geography, gender, race and party ideology:

- **geography:** 73 per cent of voters who live in inner-city areas vote Democrat
- **ethnicity:** a staggering 95 per cent of black voters voted for Obama in 2012
- **age:** Democrats attracted 60 per cent of the 18- to 29-year-old age group of voters; 57 per cent of older voters (aged 65 and over) voted Republican.

Participation in elections

White people are still the ethnic group mostly likely to vote, although the influence of ethnic-minority groups during election time is increasing. Ethnic-minority voters are now more likely to turn out than ever because of:

- **education:** people from ethnic-minority backgrounds now have better access to education and therefore they are more likely to understand the point of voting
- **better representation:** there is a great improvement in ethnic-minority representation in Congress, particularly from black and Hispanic backgrounds; Obama standing as the first black presidential candidate meant increased registration to vote and increased turnout from ethnic-minority populations
- **accessibility:** the Democrats and Republicans have tried to make voting more accessible in the Hispanic community by publishing their manifestos in Spanish as well as in English
- **high-profile celebrity campaigns:** campaigns by the likes of Samuel L. Jackson and Alicia Keys have encouraged ethnic-minority voters to see the importance of political participation; both these celebrities famously backed Obama in 2012.

The influence of ethnic-minority voters during elections

Black and Hispanic voters in particular are playing an increasing part in the outcomes of presidential elections in the USA. This is because of:

- **population size:** it is thought that the Hispanic population alone will treble by 2050 due to higher birth rates and immigration; people from ethnic minorities now make up 29 per cent of voters
- **improved registration:** this is especially true in the black community; there are also 13 million Hispanic voters (although there are thought to be a further 8 million eligible voters who have not registered)
- **the influence of immigration in swing states:** the large ethnic-minority populations in states where no single candidate or party has overwhelming support, such as Texas and California, mean that these voters are particularly influential when it comes to the outcomes of elections; politicians often target campaigns to these areas during election times
- **traditional voting patterns amongst ethnic-minority communities:** for example Asian voters tend to be Democrat – 73 per cent voted this way in 2012.

Immigration

The USA is an ethnically diverse country that was founded by immigrants. Millions of immigrants every year are attracted to the USA by the American Dream. However, immigration is a highly controversial issue and recent governments have expanded their immigration control policies. Today there is a debate between opponents of illegal immigration who are calling for tougher immigration controls and pro-immigration campaign groups who argue that immigrants are good for the economy.

Advantages of immigration

- The USA was built on immigration – immigrants bring culture and significant amounts of money to the US economy.
- In Texas and California especially, immigrants are vital to the economy. They provide cheap labour in the agricultural and hospitality sectors and keep the US economy competitive.
- In time, many immigrants earn increased wages and many are less dependent on welfare than native-born Americans.
- Many economists believe that immigrants contribute more to the economy than they cost.

Disadvantages of immigration

- Some immigrants are uneducated and unskilled and are seen as a drain on health, welfare and education systems.
- Polls show that many Americans are in favour of tighter immigration controls, such as more border guards and high security fences.
- Areas populated by different ethnic groups often experience racial tension.
- Immigration is a major issue in California and Texas – Proposition 187 was passed by Californians to deny illegal immigrants access to welfare.
- Before 9/11 immigration was an economic issue. Now it is perceived to be more of a security issue.

Social and economic inequalities

Although the USA is known as the Land of Opportunity, and it attracts millions of immigrants every year, its society is anything but equal. As a capitalist state with an economy based on boom and bust, there are always winners and losers. Anyone in America can suffer from poverty and lack opportunities, but unfortunately those from ethnic minority backgrounds are still the most likely to suffer from poverty and to have lower income levels.

Poverty and income

- In 2012, 12 per cent of white Americans lived below the poverty line. However, this figure is much higher among the black (26 per cent) and Hispanic (23 per cent) populations. Only 15 per cent of Cuban Hispanics live below the poverty line though. (Figures sourced from the Congressional Research Service.)
- In 2013, the average income for white Americans was $68,636, followed by $39,005 for Hispanic Americans and $33,321 for black Americans. Asian Americans are an economically successful ethnic minority group, earning on average $68,780 – more than white Americans on average. (Figures sourced from the US Census Bureau's Income and Poverty Report, cited in the *Wall Street Journal*, 17 September 2013.)

Healthcare

- Americans from ethnic minorities are more likely to be uninsured than white Americans. According to the US Census Bureau, 14.7 per cent of white Americans are uninsured, compared to 15 per cent of Asian, 19 per cent of black and 29 per cent of Hispanic Americans.
- Life expectancy for black and Hispanic Americans is three years less than amongst the white population: 75 years compared to 78 years.

Education

- The US Department of Education has highlighted that 81 per cent of Asian and 71 per cent of white children have access to the top science and maths courses, while only 51 per cent of black children have access to these courses.
- In some states, white students outperform black and Hispanic students by up to 26 per cent.

Housing

- In 2014, according to *Forbes Magazine*, 72 per cent of the white American population owned their own home compared to only 43 per cent of black and 45 per cent of Hispanic people.
- In 2014, 6 per cent of white people lived in inadequate housing compared to 16 per cent of the black population.

Figure 8.4 The difference between rich and poor housing areas in the USA

Government responses to social and economic inequalities

In recent years the US government has introduced a number of policies in an attempt to reduce social and economic inequalities:

- The American Recovery and Reinvestment Act (2009)
- The Affordable Care Act (2010) – otherwise known as 'Obamacare'
- Race to the Top – Equity and Opportunity (2014)

The American Recovery and Reinvestment Act (2009)

This Act promised to help those hit hardest by the recession by creating jobs and stabilising the economy. Its measures included extra funding for the Food Stamp Program, $53 billion to improve state schooling in poorer areas and $2 billion to increase the Head Start Program, which provides nutrition to poorer pupils in state schools. It also put $2 billion towards the creation of more affordable housing and $30 billion towards college scholarships for poorer families. The downside of this programme was that it added over $200 billion to the budget deficit in 2009 alone. In many respects it is too early to comment on the success of the Act, but it appears to have increased GDP by 0.5 per cent, saved an estimated 1.5 million jobs since 2010 and increased employment by 1 million people.

The Affordable Care Act (2010) – 'Obamacare'

Obamacare came fully into force in October 2013 and aimed to provide every American with affordable basic health insurance. It made it illegal to charge sicker patients more based on their pre-existing health conditions and provides free preventative care such as blood pressure checks, bowel-cancer screening for over-50s, folic acid tablets for pregnant women and HIV screening – all of which some people had to pay for in the past. It created a health insurance 'market place' where small businesses can buy cheaper healthcare plans for their employees. This policy is new and so hard to critique, but so far it seems to have made health insurance more accessible – according to the *Huffington Post*, there are an extra 8 million Americans with health insurance as a result of this policy. It has also increased access to Medicaid and Medicare. However, it is believed that 35 per cent of Americans want to see Obamacare repealed (according to *The Week*) and there are still large numbers of people, especially Hispanic people, without adequate healthcare.

Race to the Top – Equity and Opportunity (2014)

This brand-new policy is in its infancy but it is a fund of $300 million that has promised to:

- improve educational opportunities for all: government research has found that 54 per cent of people from the richest families complete college compared to only 8 per cent of those from poorer backgrounds, and this policy will aim to combat this (figures sourced from CNN News)
- reduce expulsion and drop-out rates of ethnic minority children, increase attainment in inner-city schools and increase college affordability.

Whether it is a success or not has yet to be seen.

The USA: power and international relations

Is the USA a superpower?

The USA is an extremely important world power and is widely acknowledged to be the biggest superpower. It has a huge population of 316 million people, the world's largest economy and unparalleled military might. It also has fifteen of the top twenty universities in the world, along with being extremely technologically and economically advanced.

It plays a key role in international relations and co-operation and is a member of many international organisations, such as NATO, the United Nations (UN), the G7 and the G20.

The USA and the UN

The UN is an international organisation that was set up after the Second World War to encourage international co-operation and peacekeeping. It provides aid to developing countries and plays a major role in international security. The USA was a founding member and the UN headquarters are in New York.

The USA has one of the five permanent seats on the UN Security Council, along with China, France, Russia and the UK, meaning that it is always a key player in maintaining international security. It co-operates with the other Security Council members to make decisions about world conflicts and intervention.

Case study: Conflict resolution in Syria

The USA, along with the UK and France, condemned the Assad regime in Syria and the use of chemical weapons against civilians fighting for their human rights. The USA has supplied weapons to the rebels/civilians fighting against the Syrian Government and they have voted for action against the Syrian Government in the UN Security Council. These actions have, however, been held up by China and Russia, who vetoed actions to condemn the Assad regime.

The USA, NATO and the G8

The North Atlantic Treaty Organization (NATO) is a political and military organisation that maintains international security and collective defence. It was founded in 1949, after the Second World War, and played a key role during the Cold War. Nowadays, the USA is a main player in the organisation, which has 28 member countries.

Obama's trip to Warsaw in 2014 saw him in talks with NATO to boost military protection in Eastern Europe and an additional $1 billion was funded to meet this proposal. Increasing tensions between Russia and the USA (after Russia's 'illegal' annexation of Crimea in March 2014) have led to Russia's expulsion from the G8. The leaders of the G8 met without President Putin in June 2014 to vote on economic sanctions against Russia for its 'continuing violation of Ukraine's sovereignty'.

Chapter 9

World powers: The People's Republic of China

What you should know 👍

SQA requirements

To be successful in this section, you should know about:

★ China: its political system and process:
  - ★ constitutional arrangements and the main institutions of government
  - ★ the political rights and responsibilities of citizens
  - ★ influencing the political process and opportunities for participation
  - ★ evaluating the political system and the extent of democratic influence and control

★ China: recent socio-economic issues:
  - ★ the nature and extent of socio-economic issues
  - ★ government responses to socio-economic issues
  - ★ the effectiveness of government responses to socio-economic issues

★ the role of China in international relations:
  - ★ involvement in international organisations
  - ★ relationship with other countries
  - ★ evaluating international influence and power.

Introduction

The People's Republic of China (PRC) is the fourth largest country in the world by land mass and has the largest population in the world: 1.35 billion people. The country has a very complex political, social and economic history and although its **ideology** is still communism, with strict government control and limited human rights, it has made huge steps towards becoming the fastest emerging capitalist economy in the world. The dominant ethnic group is the Han Chinese, who make up around 92 per cent of the population.

The country faces many challenges, such as rapid population growth, severe environmental pollution as a result of rapid industrialisation and maintaining the balance between economic freedom and political control.

Key word

Ideology: A set of political beliefs that guide the government of a country.

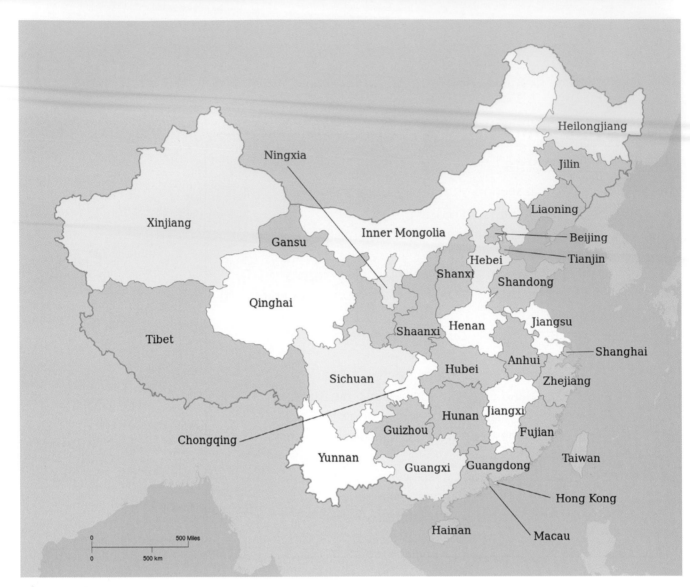

Figure 9.1 China

China's political system

China is run by the Chinese Communist Party (CCP) and has been since 1949. China is a one-party communist state with little political opposition. The government has strict controls on the population; it decides what people can access on the internet, what international politics they learn about in the classroom, what human rights they have and even how many children they can have (to an extent). The CCP claims that true representative democracy is to be found not in Western human rights but in the people's responsibility and duty to the party and nation. As such, while the Chinese Constitution highlights the extensive range of rights of Chinese people, they can only be used in conjunction with the responsibilities of citizenship as defined by the CCP.

Figure 9.2 China's leaders: President Xi Jinping and Premier Li Keqiang

The Chinese Communist Party

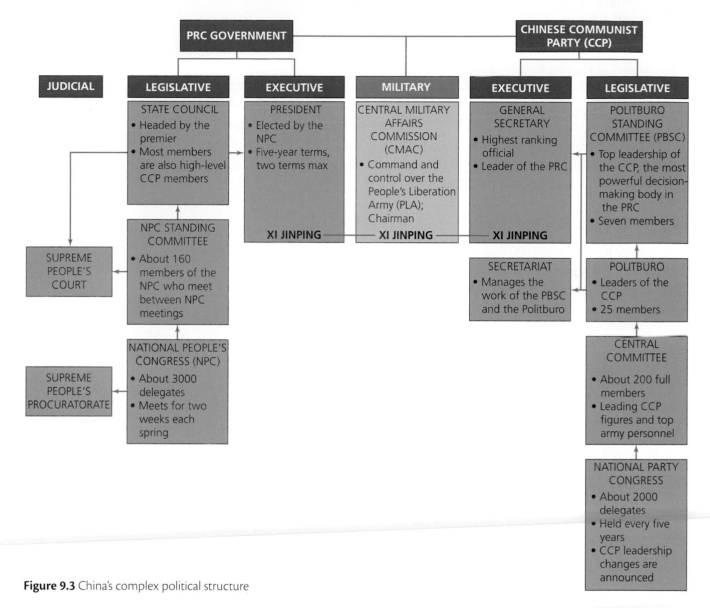

Figure 9.3 China's complex political structure

The CCP rules China from the top down under an authoritarian regime. In theory, anyone can apply to join the CCP, but in practice the membership process is competitive, rigorous and often only available to the elite or family members of current CCP members. To become a member, applicants must pass written applications, exams, interviews and a year's probation; this is all geared towards ensuring applicants' ideology matches that of the CCP and that they will be obedient to the party's beliefs. Membership is like a golden ticket to success in China; the connections and influence it provides allow better job prospects, healthcare and education for the whole family.

Many have criticised the CCP for not being representative of the population of China; there are very few women or people under 35 – although this is also the case for countries that are often viewed as more democratic than China (such as the USA and the UK). The CCP has a wide-spanning influence that dominates every aspect of people's lives: their choice of who to vote for, what they see on TV and the internet, which aspects of history and politics they learn in Chinese schools and also their rights.

The structure of the CCP is complex (see figure 9.3 on page 81), but those at the top hold the real power. The General Secretary is Xi Jinping, who is also the country's President and Military Commissioner. Below him is the Politburo Standing Committee (PBSC) of seven members who act as the President's Cabinet. This is where the main decisions for China are made – between the President and the PBSC. The head of the PBSC, and China's Premier, is Li Keqiang. Underneath this level is the Politburo of 25 members (including the seven members of the PBSC).

National Party Congress of the CCP

Not to be confused with the National People's Congress (which is China's parliament), the National Party Congress of the CCP meets once every five years. It is where major political decisions made by the CCP and the policies for China for the next five years are announced. This is known as the Five-Year Plan. It is also where members of the Politburo and PBSC are chosen.

The eighteenth National Party Congress took place in November 2012, where there was a major party overhaul: Xi Jinping took over power as the General Secretary of the CCP/President from Hu Jintao and he reduced the number of members of the PBSC from nine to seven.

The Central Military Affairs Commission (CMAC)

In an authoritarian communist country, the army plays a vital role in national security and policing the nation. In China, the People's Liberation Army (PLA) has recently been needed to maintain order during protests in Tibet. The CCP is permitted, by the Central Military Affairs Commission (CMAC), to control the PLA and China's nuclear weapons.

The CMAC has eleven members and it is their job to make decisions regarding army deployment, appointing high-ranking military personnel and arms spending. The CCP holds ultimate power over the CMAC, as Xi Jinping is also the Chairman of the CMAC.

Is power shared?
The structure of the government

The Chinese political system is dominated by the CCP. However, power is shared within the CCP more than it used to be:
- Now there is a system of 'collective leadership' where Xi Jinping and the seven members of the PBSC have different powers and advisory roles. However, most decisions are made by Xi Jinping.
- There is a written Constitution, which outlines people's rights, but it can only be used to further the interests of the state; that is, the CCP.
- The government structures – the State Council, Premier and National People's Congress – are controlled by the CCP top leadership.

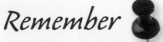

Remember

The most important institutions of the CCP are:
- ☞ the Politburo Standing Committee
- ☞ the Politburo
- ☞ the Central Military Affairs Commission.

Local politics

There are four levels of government administration: national, provincial, protectorate and county. The CCP dominates every level of government. People can vote in local village elections for the Village Committees.

Village Committees

Village Committees exist as the lowest level of government in China. Here, local people can vote for representatives and a chairperson, whose job it is to oversee local village decisions and provisions. They are elected every three years and, in 2011, 98 per cent of these representatives were directly elected by the people. It is real democratic progress in China to hold free, open elections with a secret ballot. However, there have been several criticisms of local elections, which have raised irregularities in the results and questions over how the votes have been counted. Also, the Village Committee is overseen by the Village Party Secretary from the CCP, meaning that even the Village Committees have to keep in line with CCP policy.

Political parties

On paper, China may appear to be a multi-party state, where people have a choice of different political views, but in practice this is not the case. Although eight minor 'democratic' political parties exist, they cannot be described as political opposition to the CCP, as views that differ from those of the CCP are not tolerated.

Anyone found to be starting a political party of their own faces prison or 're-education through labour'. Therefore, China can only really be considered as one-party state.

> **Remember**
>
> Only at local level can Chinese citizens vote for their representatives.

China's economy

From 1949 to the mid-1980s, China was a rigid communist country where farmers worked under a commune system (state farms) controlled by the CCP.

We can describe this system as backward:

- People worked the land and earned a wage but had no incentive to work hard.
- This system severely limited food production, individual wealth and economic growth.

This system, therefore, was overhauled in the 1980s when Deng Xiaoping introduced agricultural reforms that allowed farmers greater economic freedom. Deng stated that 'to get rich is glorious' – an unfamiliar concept in a traditionally communist Chinese economy. Many farmers, able to farm their own land, became wealthy and food production increased. Deng Xiaoping opened up China to trading with the West through the Open Door Policy, and an economically backward China began to take advantage of world markets. It joined the World Trade Organization in 2001.

The move towards a socialist capitalist market

Today:

- China has the second largest economy in the world (behind the USA)
- China is becoming more capitalist, with a modern market economy rather than its traditional state-planned and -owned economy
- there has been a huge rise in the number of multi-millionaires in China and many Chinese people have amassed huge wealth, purchasing many luxury goods with their high disposable incomes
- disposable income for the middle classes is projected to double by 2018.

However, vast social and economic inequalities now exist.

Why is China so wealthy?

Foreign direct investment (FDI)

Thousands of British and American companies have invested in China and set up businesses there. FDI increased by 5 per cent in 2013, which equated to around $117 billion. China is an appealing place to set up a business: tax breaks, a cheaper labour force, low building costs and a market of 1.3 billion people make an attractive package.

The 'factory of the world'

China still produces more products for export than any other country in the world, although its reputation as the factory of the world is beginning to reduce (due to cheaper labour appearing elsewhere in the world).

Special Economic Zones (SEZs)

First set up in 1979, SEZs are concentrated areas for businesses and factories. Rapid economic growth is prioritised to these key areas and businesses are incentivised to start up there. Perhaps the most successful is Shezhen: a fishing village 30 years ago, it is now home to nearly 16 million people, exemplifying the sheer scale of economic development and migration in China.

World leader in technology

Companies like Apple have set up in China. It is estimated that 1 billion smartphones have been sold in this country alone.

Agriculture

China produces 21 per cent of the world's food.

Increase in income

The average income in China has risen 500 per cent since 2001.

Challenges facing China's economy

The rapid industrial growth that China has undergone in recent years has had a profound social and economic impact on its population in several ways:

Migration

For the first time in its history, China's urban population now outnumbers its rural population, and millions of Chinese people migrate from rural to urban areas in search of job opportunities. Most of China's population now live on the eastern seaboard, putting pressure on housing and the social services the country provides. There are an estimated 230 million rural migrant workers in China.

Environmental damage

China is currently suffering environmentally and in terms of people's health as a result of its rapid economic expansion. According to the World Health Organization, the air quality in parts of China is considered 'hazardous' and 'unhealthy' and health ministers believe this is impacting on life expectancy in the country. China is responsible for over one-quarter of the world's greenhouse emissions.

Adequate power supplies

Highly controversial projects such as the Three Gorges Dam have been set up to overcome a lack of power supplies in China. This project officially finished in 2012 and cost $24 billion.

Social and economic inequalities

China's substantial economic revolution has led to the creation of a strong middle class (see overleaf). Freer economic policy has meant that many Chinese people can start up their own businesses for the first time and can become wealthy. China now has around 170 billionaires. The increasing middle-class population has led to a greater disposable income and, as a result, there is a growing demand for luxury goods within China itself.

However, this economic boom has not been experienced equally by everyone. Many migrant workers, who move to urban areas in search of jobs, work extremely long hours for very little pay. China's movement towards capitalism has created one of the most unequal societies in the world. President Xi Jinping said that 'the most arduous and heavy task facing China in completing the building of a moderately prosperous society is in rural areas, especially poverty-stricken regions'.

Employment and income

China's average income for 2014 was around $7000 a year per person. The government's overdevelopment and investment in the east of the country, while overlooking the development needs of the west of China, has led to unequal economic growth. Therefore, income levels and employment opportunities vary wildly in different parts of the country. Those who live in rural areas have very few job opportunities and still tend to work in the agricultural or mining sectors, both of which pay very poorly. In comparison, those who live in urban areas earn around three times as much as those in rural areas, and the attraction of the city pulls many migrants from rural to urban areas, especially to SEZs.

The 'floating population'

China's rural-to-urban economic migrants are often referred to as the 'floating population' as they have no fixed abode and divide their time between working in urban areas for most of the year and returning home for brief family visits. Around 230 million people from rural areas work in the cities. This floating population is expected to continue to grow at an alarming rate, with around 300 million additional people anticipated to move to urban areas in the next 30 years (www.china.org.cn). This has created a number of social and economic problems in urban areas, such as overcrowding and a lack of affordable housing and social services.

The middle class

China's class structure has changed in recent years and there is now a larger middle class in China than ever before. This is because the move towards a capitalist economy has allowed:

- people to start their own businesses
- more jobs to be created in service industries such as telecommunications, insurance, banking and technology
- people to have a higher disposable income; that is, extra money to spend on luxuries.

The middle-class population in China tends to be categorised as those who have a university degree, a professional degree and an above-average income.

Healthcare

The healthcare system is reliant on a person having health insurance, which is usually paid for by individuals, often alongside employer contributions. As the system is insurance based, and therefore reliant on income, it has inherent inequalities. The system itself is run by the National Health and Family Planning Commission, which has a Bureau of Health in every province.

Government responses to improve healthcare

The CCP has aimed to improve healthcare in China by:

- setting improvement targets in the twelfth Five-Year Plan, such as to improve rural healthcare facilities and to invest more money into the healthcare system – a total of $371 billion
- planning to introduce universal healthcare by 2020, known as the Healthy 2020 Strategy
- improving access to healthcare: the Social Insurance Law means that health coverage rates have increased by 65 per cent between 2003 and 2012.

These measures have resulted in a reduction in the infant mortality rates (IMR) and a rise in life expectancy.

China's health problems

China's healthcare system faces many challenges that can be attributed to lifestyle choices brought on by higher incomes and economic growth:

- **Obesity:** A rise in disposable income and the Western influence of fast food have meant that 92 million people in China now have type 2 diabetes, and many more people are suffering from heart disease than in the past.
- **Smoking:** Up to 61 per cent of Chinese men smoke, which is one of the highest figures in the world, and around 30 per cent of the world's smokers live in China. This has an extremely adverse effect on the population's health, increasing the risks of cancers and strokes.

However, the system still has its flaws:

- The healthcare system is still only ranked 144th in the world.
- Patients at the moment still have to pay for around one-third of their care.
- Doctors may be corrupt as many are paid by the drug companies to prescribe unnecessary medication to their patients.
- China's health problems are increasing, for example obesity.

Education

Schooling in China is provided by the state, although private schools exist and are popular in wealthy, urban communities. China's education is internationally renowned and regarded as competitive and academically challenging. Everyone in China is supposed to receive nine years' mandatory education, although in reality this is not always the case, and once again disparities between rural and urban communities are very stark: while 80 per cent of urban students graduate from high school, only 20 per cent of rural students do so (also see below).

Government responses to improve education

The government has tried to improve education in China by:

- increasing the focus on technology and science to improve China's service industries
- improving pre-school education
- making the education system more equal: the government has been increasing investment in rural schools, which tend to be poorly resourced
- increasing educational spending.

However, China's education system is still far from equal and inherent inequalities persist, particularly between rural and urban schools. Teachers in some rural areas are paid only half of what those in high-attaining urban schools receive. Teachers in rural areas are given fewer training opportunities and fewer resources. Rural drop-out rates are far higher than urban ones. Finally, only 5 per cent of rural teenagers go on to university compared to 84 per cent of teenagers in Shanghai.

Housing

Housing in China varies enormously, but the biggest deciding factor in the standard of housing a person lives in is personal wealth. There is an urban–rural divide to a certain degree, but those who live in the cities may also live in poor, substandard housing. Although those who live in rural areas are more likely to suffer substandard

Figure 9.4 Economically developed Shanghai

housing that may lack access even to electricity and water, urban life is no guarantee of decent housing: Many people now live in 'urban villages' where villages, which were once in the countryside, have been swallowed up on all sides by the emerging suburbs of ever-expanding cities. This engulfing of villages by cities leads to a disparity within the new urban area. Although the city has brand new buildings and apartments, the village attached to it is more like a slum or ghetto and becomes a breeding ground for crime and cheap migrant housing.

In comparison, wealthy citizens live in gated communities and lucrative studio apartments. Their homes are designed for them and interior decorators are drafted in to create luxurious 'pads'. Shanghai alone is home to 166,000 millionaires.

Government responses to improve housing

Once again, the government has outlined solutions to the housing crisis in China in its recent twelfth Five-Year Plan:

- The government aims to create 36 million more affordable homes in city areas. This is to control spiralling housing costs in the cities.
- It has relaxed housing regulations under the Hukou to allow for more freedom of the workforce and therefore access to housing.

Figure 9.5 Overcrowding in China's urban villages

However, China's housing system has the following problems:

- Mass migration, leading to a lack of affordable housing. Many migrant workers have no option but to rent rooms in 'urban villages', which are ghetto areas associated with crime and poor life chances.
- Rising house prices in areas such as Shanghai, which has seen house-price rises of 25 per cent in 2013 alone. It is hard for people to afford homes in the current global housing crisis faced by many developed countries.

Political rights in China

Chinese people have a number of political rights and responsibilities, as shown in Table 9.1.

Rights	Responsibilities
To vote in local village elections	To turn out to vote
To submit petitions to the Chinese Government (the 2013 e-petitions website allows this)	To fill out their name, address and passport number for identification, to ensure names are not made up
To hold protests/demonstrations	To ask the permission of the government first and act peacefully
To join the CCP	To apply properly and follow the code of the CCP

Table 9.1 Political rights in China

The CCP has very strict control over every aspect of life in China, leading countries like the UK to criticise China for its human rights record. The Chinese people have limited right to free speech, freedom of religion and political opposition, as ideas against CCP beliefs are not tolerated. However, new business opportunities and property rights are beginning to give Chinese people more economic freedoms.

Internet control

According to the *Washington Post*, there were 618 million internet users in China in 2014. This has led to:

- an increase in 'cyber democracy', where people anonymously post criticisms of the CCP (sourced from Emory University thesis); the CCP has responded by applying extreme methods of censorship
- the 'Great Firewall of China': the government bans Chinese people from accessing any websites that may be too 'westernised', for example BBC News, Amnesty International and Facebook
- the government employing thousands of internet police and even paying bloggers to write articles that give a positive spin on the work of the CCP
- the continual monitoring of TV: Chinese people are unable to watch Westernised shows like *The Big Bang Theory* and arrests over internet protests are common.

Freedom of religion

According to Article 36 of the Constitution, Chinese citizens should have the right to practise their chosen religion. However:

- members of the Falun Gong religion face prosecution and persecution – over 3000 have been killed since practising Falun Gong was banned by the government in 1999 and tens of thousands of people are locked up in Laogai camps (see below)
- the government has started to become wary of Christian mega-churches (large churches with thousands of followers) and shut down several in Wenzhou in 2014 because they are 'illegal'; in addition, no church meetings can be held outside the church or registered building.

Human rights in Tibet and Xinjiang

Both of these areas of China are autonomous regions, but many people in these areas wish for full independence from Chinese rule. The Chinese Government views Tibet as ruled from Beijing, but many people in the region wish to see Tibet as a free state. It is a similar case in Xinjiang where many Muslims in the area feel marginalised by Chinese rule and wish for independence for the region. This has led to several bloody uprisings, protests and up to 120 examples of self-immolation (setting oneself on fire in protest, leading to death) in Tibet.

Laogai camps

The aim of this system is to 're-educate people through labour'; that is, people who disagree with the CCP's beliefs may be arrested and taken to a labour camp. This system has several sections, and prisoners are forced to manufacture goods for export. This labour force has contributed to China's wealth but people are held and made to work against their will.

Laojiao camps are where people are 're-educated', often through torture, to ensure that they change their views in favour of the CCP.

Over 1000 Laogai camps still exist, with an estimated 3–5 million people currently held against their will. However, in December 2013 the Chinese Government said it will be reviewing and possibly abolishing these camps, although it is too soon to tell if this will happen.

Death penalty

China still executes more people every year than the rest of the world combined. The actual number of executions is never published by the government, but it is estimated to be around about 5000 a year. A total of 55 crimes still carry the death penalty (although this has recently been reduced from 68) – something that has been widely criticised and condemned by nations around the world.

One-child policy

An improvement in human rights in China can be seen in the relaxing of the one-child policy. Now families can:
- have more than one child if either parent was an only child themselves
- have a second child if the first is a girl if they live in rural areas, where restrictions are less strict.

However, human rights issues still exist; many people still face forced abortions, sterilisation and hefty fines for breaking family-planning rules.

China's international role

Is China a superpower?

Many people claim that China is an emerging superpower because:
- it has the world's largest population (1.3 billion people)
- it has the second largest economy in the world and is the world's largest exporter
- it has a massive annual economic growth rate of 7 per cent per annum
- it is a member of many key international organisations, such as the UN and the G20.

However, many people would not consider China to be a superpower as it lacks the military capabilities of other superpowers such as the USA.

China and the UN

The People's Republic of China has been a member of the UN since 1971 and plays a key role by:

- holding one of the five permanent seats on the UN Security Council (along with France, the UK, the USA and Russia)
- being an important part of UN agencies such as UNEP (the United Nations Environment Programme) and has promised to reduce its carbon dioxide emissions
- providing 6.5 per cent of the UN's peacekeeping budget
- providing assistance to fight international terrorist groups such as Boko Haram
- being heavily involved in peacekeeping missions in Mali in 2014.

However, China has had disputes with other countries, such as:

- territorial disagreements with the Philippines, Japan and Vietnam over areas of the South China Sea
- Russia and China both vetoed the UN's action plan for Syria, which France, the UK and the USA agreed should go ahead.

China and the G20

China is one of the main members of the Group of Twenty, or G20, countries. It has recently been heavily involved in:

- talks on how to solve the world financial crisis
- implementing measures to improve international economic stability.

As one of the richest countries in the world, it continues to dominate world economic affairs.

Relationships with other countries: China and the UK

Both Alex Salmond and David Cameron have held high-profile meetings with Xi Jinping in China and the UK. The UK works closely with China to:

- improve cultural links: there are now over 200 annual events that promote the UK's culture in China; also, the number of Chinese students in Scotland has risen to 7000
- improve economic ties: the UK has benefited from economic ties with China; Scottish exports to China have now reached £500 million annually and over 1500 jobs have been created in Britain as a result of working alongside Chinese companies.

World powers: The Republic of South Africa

Introduction

South Africa is a multiracial democracy based on a written constitution that includes a Bill of Rights. The country is a relatively new democracy as it was only in 1994 that the domination of the white minority ended (the apartheid system). In the first free multiracial elections, Nelson Mandela, leader of the African National Congress (ANC), became the first president of the new 'Rainbow Nation'.

South Africa is the richest country in southern Africa and the region's superpower. It is rich in natural resources and has a modern manufacturing industry, although the economic recession in the developed world has weakened its economy.

Figure 10.1 Nelson Mandela, father of the new South Africa, died in December 2013 and a nation mourned

Over 20 years on from the end of white rule, the **legacy of apartheid** remains, as indicated by the words of Archbishop Desmond Tutu in 1994:

'Apartheid has left a ghastly legacy. There is a horrendous housing shortage and high unemployment, healthcare is not easily affordable by the majority; Bantu [Black African] education has left us with a massive educational crisis; there is gross maldistribution of wealth.'

> ## Key word
>
> **Legacy of apartheid:** The social and economic inequalities that still exist today between the races as a result of white rule (1948–94) that separated the races (apartheid) and denied non-white people their political, social and economic rights.

Population

South Africa has a population of more than 52 million people made up of the following racial groups. Its citizens are referred to as the Rainbow Nation because of these racial groups and tribal identities (see Figure 10.2). There are eleven official languages.

Black African

Black Africans make up almost 80 per cent of the population. The main tribal groups are Xhosa and Zulu. The black African population has increased from 74 per cent in 1994 to 79 per cent in 2014 due to a higher birth rate and white migration.

Coloured

The coloured ethnic group is made up of people of mixed race who in the 2011 Census became the second largest ethnic group, overtaking the white population. Most people from this group live in the Northern and Western Cape.

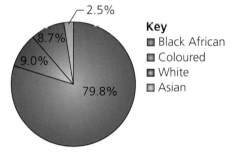

Figure 10.2 Population groupings in South Africa by percentage in 2013

White

The white population is declining and is now less than 10 per cent of the total population. White South Africans can be divided into two groups: English-speaking and Afrikaans-speaking. The Afrikaners ruled the country from 1948–94 under the policy of apartheid. Many of the Afrikaners are farmers and regard themselves as the 'white tribe' of South Africa.

Asian

This population was brought to South Africa by the British in the nineteenth century and is the smallest racial group.

Key political issues

To what extent is South Africa a successive and stable democracy, rather than a country moving towards being a one-party state?

South Africa: a political success story?

South Africa is a successive and stable democracy with free elections at all levels of government based on the Party List system of proportional representation. A free press exists and citizens can criticise actions of the government and join a political party, pressure group and/or a trade union.

The Constitution

South Africa has a written Constitution that guarantees its people an extensive range of human rights. The Constitution makes clear reference to the need to address the inequalities created by apartheid. Article 9.2 states:

'To promote achievement of equality, legislative and other measures designed to protect or advance categories of persons disadvantaged by unfair discrimination may be taken.'

This has enabled the ANC Government to pass legislation that discriminates against white people (see page 101), to further its goal of **Black Transformation**.

The Constitution provides for an independent judiciary. The Constitutional Court is the highest court of the land, and deals with the interpretation, protection and enforcement of the Constitution. One of its most famous decisions was to order the government of then President Mbeki to provide anti-HIV/AIDS drugs free of charge to mothers who have HIV/AIDS and their babies at birth.

However, the dominance of the ANC has led to some critics stating that the country is moving towards a one-party state. Corruption is a major problem in South Africa. President Zuma has been criticised for building a vast homestead that will cost South African citizens R328 million (around £18 million).

Main institutions of government

South Africa has a bicameral parliament, consisting of a National Assembly (400 members) and the National Council of Provinces (NCOP). Elections for both houses are held every five years and are based on a system of proportional representation. The president is elected by the National Assembly from among its members and he/she is the executive head of state and also appoints the Cabinet. The president may not serve more than two five-year terms in office. The dominance of the ANC ensures that the leader of the ANC becomes president.

South Africa is divided into nine provinces (see Figure 10.3), each with its own provincial government and premier. Eight of the nine provinces are controlled by the ANC and President Zuma uses his power of patronage to appoint the respective eight premiers. The Constitution offers limited powers to the provinces and their function is to implement the policies of the National Government. The Democratic Alliance, which controls the Western Cape, has been successful in delivering local services.

> **Key word**
>
> **Black Transformation:** Government legislation to ensure that senior posts in the public and private sector and the allocation of government works contracts reflect the racial composition of South Africa.

'When he [Zuma] was elected President of the ANC (2007), he had more than 700 criminal cases – including corruption – hanging over his head. The charges were dropped by the NPA, which meant that not one of these cases was dismissed by a court of law … With Zuma at the top, the ANC keeps the acronym but has acquired an unenviable image and different wording: Alleged National Criminal organisation.'

Extract from *The Fall of the ANC* by Prince Mashele and Mzukisi Qobo, 2014

There are over 280 local councils, referred to as municipalities, and large cities such as Cape Town and Johannesburg have their own councils. Many councils are failing to deliver basic services such as refuge collection and school transport.

Participation opportunities

Apart from voting and being a member of a political party, South Africans can join pressure groups, including trade unions and community groups. One pressure group known as Section 27 is taking the government to court for failing to deliver school textbooks. Unfortunately, many local groups have lost confidence in their politicians and resort to illegal protests that in many cases become violent. Virtually every day in South Africa a violent protest occurs, especially in the townships denied the amenities promised by the government, for example residents in an informal settlement in Gauteng barricaded roads with burning tyres in protest at the lack of running water, electricity and sanitation. Many South Africans do not trust the police, and events such as the Marikana massacre of 2012 reinforce the view that official trade unions and the police are there to serve the ANC and not the people.

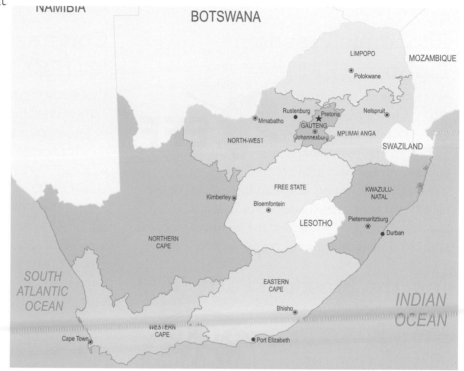

Figure 10.3 South Africa and its nine provinces

Political parties

African National Congress (ANC)

The ANC dominates South African politics and is the party of Nelson Mandela and black liberation. It has won all five of the national elections

and, despite the cloud of corruption hanging over President Zuma, it won over 60 per cent of votes and 249 seats in 2014. Black African people, especially the poor and poorly educated, remain loyal to the ANC.

National Freedom Party (NFP)

Zenele kaMagwaza-Msibi, former chairperson of Inkatha Freedom Party (IFP), set up the NFP in 2011 with other former IFP members, thus weakening the IFP. The NFP won six seats in the 2014 National Election

and in the provincial elections in KwaZulu-Natal it gained six seats.

$\Rightarrow$

Democratic Alliance (DA)

The DA is the second largest party, with 89 seats, and in the 2014 National Election it retained control of the Western Cape. The DA has increased its support in every general election. Its main supporters are white, mixed-race and Asian people. It now has support of a growing number of black African voters.

Economic Freedom Fighters (EFF)

Julius Malema, the former ANC Youth leader, formed EFF in October 2013 and gained an impressive 6.4 per cent of the votes in the 2014 National Election. EFF won the support of the far left and young disillusioned black African voters. It advocates nationalisation of the mining sector and land redistribution without compensation.

Inkatha Freedom Party (IFP)

The IFP, led by Chief Buthelezi, draws its support largely from Zulu-speaking South Africans. It wants greater powers to be given to the provinces. It is a party in decline, and lost heavily to the ANC in the 2009 National Election in KwaZulu-Natal, and in the 2014 National Election the party only won ten seats.

United Democratic Movement (UDM)

The UDM was formed in 1997 and has witnessed a steady decline since the 1999 National Election. Its leader is a former member of the ANC, Bantu Holmisa. Its power base is the Eastern Cape, where it came third in the 2014 Provincial Elections. It won four seats in the National Election in 2014.

Congress of the People (COPE)

This is a new political party, formed in 2008 by former Xhosa members of the ANC who had supported Thabo Mbeki. It came third in the 2009 National Election but failed to win enough support from black African voters to challenge the ANC. It is now a party divided and in decline, with only three MPs.

Elections

National elections are held every five years under a proportional representation system, which closely matches votes to seats won by a political party. The formation of new parties is encouraged: four new political parties contested the 2014 National Election for the first time – NFP, EFF, Agang South Africa and African Independent Congress. This weakens opposition to the ANC as new parties divide the opposition. The use of a Party List system means that the loyalty of ANC MPs is to the party and not to the people, as there are no constituency links to the electorate.

Hints & tips ★

You should be aware of both the strengths and the weaknesses of the South African PR Party List system. Can you list two advantages and two disadvantages of this system for the South African electorate?

Voter turnout of those registered to vote was a healthy 73.4 per cent in 2014, down from the 77.3 per cent of the 2009 National Election. However, these figures exclude the millions who failed to register. Only one-third of those aged 18 to 19 – the 'born-free' generation – voted.

The 2014 National Election

As expected, the ANC won the National Election with a clear majority – 62 per cent of the votes. However, it was the smallest percentage it has achieved in the five elections held since 1994, though the victory was still impressive and displayed the affection for Mandela's party by the black African population. Despite widespread ANC corruption, an economy with slow growth and massive unemployment, most black Africans voted with their hearts and not their heads. About 44 per cent of households depend on welfare payments to make ends meet, and the ANC has been criticised for using political rallies to give out state-funded food parcels to those who turn up.

The DA, with 22 per cent of the votes, achieved its best ever result, and more importantly it retained control of the Western Cape and significantly increased its support in Gauteng, gaining 30 per cent of the vote there. In total, the DA obtained over 4 million votes, compared to its previous high of just under 3 million in 2009. It is clear that the DA is widening its support to include educated and middle-class black African voters.

The EFF became the third largest party, with 25 MPs in the national parliament. Significantly, it came second in two of the poorer provinces – Limpopo and North West. With a million votes, EFF hopes to win further support from unemployed and poverty-stricken citizens.

Party	2004		2009		2014	
	Seats	Votes (%)	Seats	Votes (%)	Seats	Votes (%)
African National Congress	279	69.9	264	65.9	249	62.1
Democratic Alliance	50	12.6	67	16.7	89	22.2
Inkatha Freedom Party	28	6.9	18	4.5	10	2.4
Congress of the People	–	–	30	7.4	3	0.7
Economic Freedom Fighters	–	–	–	–	25	6.3

Table 10.1 National Assembly election results for the main political parties: 2004, 2009 and 2014

To what extent is South Africa a successful democracy?

Arguments for	Arguments against
South Africa is a stable model of democracy for Africa. There have been five peaceful elections based on PR. In the 2014 National Election, 28 political parties participated, with 13 parties now sitting in the National Assembly.	There is a fear that South Africa is becoming a one-party state. The ANC has won all five post-apartheid elections convincingly and controls eight of the nine provinces. Only in Western Cape is it in opposition.
South Africa has a federal system of government, with powers divided between central and provincial governments.	The federal system exists only on paper. Provinces must implement the policies of the national government, such as BEE (Black Economic Empowerment) legislation.
South Africa has a liberal Constitution that guarantees freedom to its citizens. It provides for an independent judiciary. The Constitutional Court ordered Mbeki to provide drugs to combat HIV/AIDS.	The policy of transformation politics could threaten the independence of judges and the rights of non-black South Africans. Jacob Zuma regards judges as 'arrogant' and ignoring the will of the people (the ANC).
There is a free press and civil society able to criticise and monitor the actions of the government. The success of the Truth and Reconciliation Commission highlights the openness of South African society.	The South African Broadcasting Corporation (SABC) is regarded as the mouthpiece of the ANC. In 2014 it refused to run DA and EFF political adverts as they criticised the ANC. A government 'Secrecy Bill' threatens the independence of the press.
A peaceful transition from Mandela to Mbeki occurred. Likewise, the power struggle between Thabo Mbeki and Jacob Zuma was resolved peacefully with the resignation of Mbeki as president in September 2008.	There is an issue of corruption, with leading ANC members being sent to jail. President Zuma's vast homestead, built at the cost of R328 million (around £18 million) of taxpayers' money, highlights the arrogance and greed of ANC leaders.

Table 10.2 Arguments for and against South Africa being a successful democracy

Social and economic issues

Key issue

To what extent has the government been successful in reducing social and economic inequalities?

Education

Progress

- In 2014, the government invested 21 per cent of its entire budget in education (6 per cent of GNP).
- Segregated education has ended and extra funding is given to poorer schools.
- Progress has been made in reducing to 40 per cent the number of schools with no sanitation, water or electricity.
- Black South Africans now make up 65 per cent of students in higher education.
- Grade 12 matriculation results (equivalent to the Scottish Higher) have improved significantly. In 1996 the pass rate was 48.9 per cent; by 2013 it had risen to 70 per cent.
- Free education has been expanded to enable students in poor urban and rural areas to attend school. Attendance figures have increased from 0.7 per cent in 2002 to 55 per cent in 2013. These same students receive a nutritional lunch (the 'Mandela sandwich').

- The number of adults with literacy problems has decreased. The *Kha Ri Gude Mass Literacy Campaign* involved more than 2 million people between 2009 and 2013.

Problems

- The education system is still in crisis. The Swiss-based World Economic Forum ranks South Africa 146th out of 148 countries – and last in mathematics and science.
- Only four students in ten who begin school stay to pass the matriculation exams. In the Department of Basic Education's numeracy test, only 12 per cent of 12-year-olds scored above the minimum proficiency.
- Substantial inequalities exist between the provinces in terms of provision. In the Western Cape, 96 per cent of schools have electricity, whereas in the Eastern Cape that figure is only 60 per cent.
- Substantial inequalities exist between the provinces in terms of exam results. In Gauteng the pass rate is over 78 per cent, whereas in Limpopo it is 58 per cent.
- The schools with the poorest facilities and results are the schools in townships or rural communities. About 80 per cent of white children complete the final year of high school, compared to less than 40 per cent of black students.
- Standards of teaching are low, especially in maths and science. In challenging schools there is a shortage of qualified teachers and a culture of non-learning.

Health

Progress

- A free healthcare programme for children under six and pregnant women has been implemented.
- Immunisation against diseases such as polio and tuberculosis is free for all children under the age of six.
- Twelve state-of-the-art hospitals have been built.
- Over 2 million South Africans now receive anti-HIV/AIDS drugs.
- Availability of clean water to millions of South Africans has been a key weapon against illness and disease.

Problems

- A shortage of doctors and nurses places a strain on the health service.
- The HIV/AIDS epidemic has led to a decline in life expectancy, which had dropped from 62 in the 1980s to 52 in 2006. It has now risen to 56.
- Provinces that recorded the highest HIV/AIDS prevalence were KwaZulu-Natal (37.4 per cent), Mpumalanga (36.7 per cent) and Free State (32.5 per cent). The Northern Cape and Western Cape recorded the lowest prevalence at 17.0 per cent and 18.2 per cent respectively.
- UNAIDS estimated that around 5.6 million South Africans were living with HIV at the end of 2013, including 460,000 children under 15 years old.

Housing and land

Progress

- Since 1994, the government has built over 4 million homes with access to electricity. Soweto is an example of a once-poor township of over a million people that now boasts a shopping mall and up-market housing.
- More than 90 per cent of households have access to running water and 85 per cent to electricity. Millions of South Africans who once lived isolated in darkness in forgotten black African communities have electricity.
- Around 80 per cent of households have a television, an electric stove and access to a mobile phone.
- Over 70,000 land distribution claims have been settled.
- Many different races now live in the same residential areas, reflecting the Rainbow Nation.

Problems

- The influx of rural populations to urban areas has led to the creation of thousands of informal settlements (squatter camps) that lack electricity and sanitation provision.
- Gauteng and North West have the largest numbers of informal settlements, with one in five of their citizens trapped in these poverty zones.
- Crime, unemployment and drug use are major problems in the townships and informal settlements.
- Regional inequalities still persist. Although 98 per cent of households in the Western Cape have access to piped water, this figure is only 60 per cent in Limpopo.
- For black African people trapped in informal settlements, racial segregation is still a reality.

Wealth and employment

Progress

- Thanks in part to affirmative action legislation, most black African people are better off than they were in 1994, either because of higher paid employment or because of the massive increase in welfare payments to the poor (social grants). The number who receive welfare grants has risen from 2.6 million to 16 million.
- The social grants system is the largest form of government support for people living in poverty. Most is given in the form of a child-support grant, which reached 8.2 million families in 2012 compared to only 80,000 in 2001.
- Between 1997 and 2011, the proportion living on less than $2 a day fell from 12 per cent to 5 per cent.
- The majority of black African people now have bank accounts, compared to one in five twenty years ago.
- Around 40 per cent of senior managers are now from the black African population, compared to about 4 per cent in 1994.

Problems

- The wealth gap has widened in South Africa since the enforcement of Black Economic Empowerment (BEE) legislation. The GINI coefficient, which measures inequality in society, was 0.59 in 1994; today it is 0.69.
- Unequal education creates unequal employment. The official unemployment rate among white people is 7 per cent compared to 30 per cent for black African people.
- Black African youth unemployment has risen to 50 per cent; white youth unemployment is about 15 per cent.
- A new term has been coined – tenderpreneurs – that refers to black African people who get rich from winning government contracts from politicians happy to accept cash for favours: corruption is still rife.

Statistics from www.bbc.co.uk

Affirmative action (positive discrimination) legislation

To achieve Black Transformation (see page 94), the government uses positive discrimination legislation to set racial quotas for entry to higher education, public and private sector employment and the allocation of government contracts.

BEE legislation, including the Employment Equity Act, is enforced to ensure that employment, especially senior management posts, reflects the racial balance of society. This has led to the creation of a wealthy black middle class referred to as **Black Diamonds**. Many white people argue that reverse racism now exists. Critics of BEE legislation argue that it has helped only a small group of black African people while the majority have seen limited benefits.

> **Key word**
>
> **Black Diamonds:** This new black elite of over 3 million now fills top posts in the public and private sectors. They live in the wealthiest suburbs of South Africa's cities beside their white neighbours. Their children go to the best state schools or to private schools and they have private health insurance to ensure the best medical treatment.

Crime and the law

The fear and impact of crime is one issue that unites all races. The defence offered by the famous disabled athlete Oscar Pistorius for shooting dead his girlfriend in 2013 – that there was an intruder in his bathroom – is an occurrence feared by all.

Despite the official murder rate falling from an average of 55 a day to 44, South Africa still has one of the highest murder rates in the world. The Democratic Alliance claims that many crimes are not reported to the police as the public have little faith in the culprits being apprehended; police corruption and brutality are also major issues, with the last two National Police Commissioners being arrested on charges of corruption. The investigation into the Marikana massacre raised issues that the police had a shoot-to-kill directive towards the striking miners. A 2013 opinion poll showed that two-thirds of South Africans think the most corrupt officials are found in the police.

> **Hints & tips** ⭐
>
> *Remember that key social issues are health, housing and education; economic issues are living standards, employment and unemployment and wealth inequalities. Social and economic issues are of course linked: if you have a high living standard you will live in a nice area.*

Key issue

To what extent does South Africa have influence in international relations?

South Africa and international influence

South Africa is an active member of the United Nations. The country was elected in 2006 and in 2010 by the UN General Assembly to serve on the Security Council. South Africa's role has been criticised by the West for placing its loyalties with the countries of the developing world ahead of human rights issues. In particular, a 'no' security vote on a resolution criticising the Burmese government, and South Africa's original intention to vote against economic sanctions to be imposed on Iran, attracted widespread criticism.

South Africa is the only country in sub-Saharan Africa to be a member of the G20, and the only African nation to have hosted the football World Cup finals, which took place in 2010.

Under the apartheid era (1948–90), South Africa experienced international isolation. Following the abolition of apartheid, the stature of Nelson Mandela ensured that the new South Africa would play a leading role among the countries of the developing world and in international organisations such as the African Union and NEPAD. Nkosazana Dlamini-Zuma, a leading member of the ANC in South Africa, was elected chairwoman of the **African Union (AU)**, highlighting South Africa's influence in the organisation.

South Africa has played a central role in seeking to end various African conflicts in Burundi, Democratic Republic of the Congo, Comoros and, more controversially, in Zimbabwe.

South Africa is a member of the BRICS (Brazil, Russia, India, China and South Africa) bloc, and is playing an important role in the shifting and distribution of power internationally. The BRICS bloc represents 43 per cent of the world's population and approximately one-fifth of global gross domestic product (GDP). South Africa sees its role in BRICS as promoting the African agenda. As President Jacob Zuma stated: 'Our belief is that the membership of South Africa to BRICS represents the 1 billion people on the continent of Africa.'

South Africa – a regional superpower?

With one-third of the GDP of sub-Saharan Africa and two-thirds of that of the Southern African Development Community (SADC), the South African economy is the driving force of southern African development. However, Nigeria is now challenging South Africa's economic dominance. In April 2014, under revised GDP figures, Nigeria passed South Africa to become the biggest economy in Africa. Although, based on population size, South Africa's GDP per capita is way above Nigeria's (see Table 10.3), in August 2014 the South African economy was classified as in recession. Nigeria's internal problems, such as the Islamist militant group Boko Haram, have exposed the weakness of the Nigerian government and division in society.

> ### Key word
>
> **African Union (AU):**
> A union consisting of 54 African states whose role is to provide 'African solutions to African problems', to support economic growth and to achieve conflict resolutions between states.

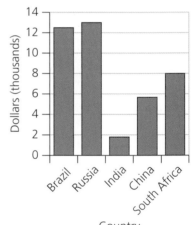

Figure 10.4 BRICS countries' GDP per capita, 2014

	Nigeria	South Africa
GDP growth	6.0%	2.5–3.0%
GDP per capita	$2800	$8000

Table 10.3 Nigeria and South Africa: GDP growth and GDP per capita, 2014

Chapter 11
World issues: Development in Africa

SQA requirements

To be successful in this section, you should know about:

★ what development is and why there is a lack of development in some African countries

★ the social, economic and political factors that hinder development in Africa and to what extent each factor hinders development

★ the impact a lack of development has on individuals, countries and their governments

★ the attempts made by national, regional and international organisations to resolve development issues in Africa.

Defining development

A developed country is a country that can well look after itself; it has a strong, stable government, citizens can access social services such as education and healthcare and it is financially stable due to fair trade. People in a developed country have the opportunity to live long, healthy lives and better themselves through education and employment. However, this is not the case for all countries around the world, and while countries such as the UK and the USA are well-developed nations, other countries in areas such as Africa are still developing.

Africa the continent

Africa is a continent of over 50 countries and, like any continent, there are areas that are rich and others that are poor. The continent suffers from various problems that affect its development, many of which stem from its time of colonialism, when many African countries were owned by other nations, who used their vast mineral and food resources and left them under-developed. There are about 1 billion people in Africa and it contains the top fifteen most under-developed countries in the world. Around 70 per cent of people in Africa live on less than $2 a day.

We shall focus on sub-Saharan Africa, where social, economic and political problems differ from those in the north of Africa.

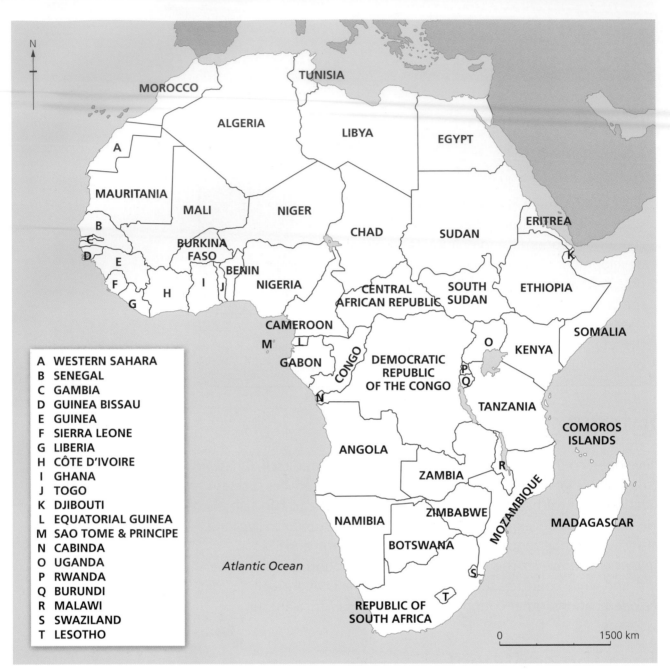

Figure 11.1 Africa

Measuring development

Development can be measured by development indicators, which are used to show a country's social and economic progress (see Table 11.1).

A high infant mortality rate (IMR) can show a lot about a country's healthcare system or access to basic healthcare. In African countries, healthcare provisions are often too expensive for people to afford or are badly under-resourced, leading to a higher IMR. Low literacy rates show that access to education is poor or that the quality of education received is sub-standard.

Developed country	Developing country
Low infant mortality rate	High infant mortality rate
High literacy rate	Low literacy rate
Low birth rate	High birth rate
High levels of primary school attendance	Low levels of primary school attendance

Table 11.1 Development indicators: developed and developing countries

Factors hindering development

Many countries in Africa suffer from a combination of social, economic and political factors that hinder overall development. These can include those shown in Table 11.2.

Social	Economic	Political
Lack of healthcare	Cash crops	Conflict
Poor access to education	Trade	Bad government/kleptocracy/corruption

Table 11.2 Factors that influence development in Africa

Although these factors can be identified separately as social, economic or political, they are all interlinked, and one issue tends to have a knock-on effect on the others, for example dictatorship or bad government can lead to a lack of social services like education and healthcare.

Healthcare in Africa

Africa is rife with health problems such as malaria, cholera and HIV/AIDS. Although drugs are available to treat malaria and suppress HIV/AIDS, they are not readily available to people and they are too expensive for most families to afford. Hospitals tend to be poorly resourced and staffed and they are in cities too far away from people living in towns or rural areas. Over 70 per cent of people infected with HIV/AIDS in the world live in Africa, and the World Health Organization estimates that 25 million people in Africa have HIV/AIDS. It kills 1.5 million people in that continent every year; that is, 6300 a day. This has a huge impact on society as it dramatically lowers life expectancy and prevents people from working the land or receiving an education.

Case study: HIV/AIDS in Swaziland

Swaziland has the highest prevalence of HIV/AIDS of any country in the world. Over 26 per cent of the population is HIV positive and this is severely affecting development in the region. There are over 75,000 orphans in the country who have lost their parents to the disease. This has dramatically reduced the number of farmers in the area, as the illness often affects people of working age. It is thought that the illness may kill up to 15 per cent of the country's farmers, making food shortages a real likelihood. The transmission of HIV has been an ongoing issue in a country where access to sexual health information and contraception are very difficult to find.

Case study: Malaria

- 88 per cent of the world's malaria deaths every year happen in Africa.
- Anti-malaria sprays have been applied to houses in some areas of countries such as Uganda, and this is 80 per cent effective in combating malaria. However, this has caused problems for farmers in the area who specialise in growing organic fruit and vegetables – the anti-malaria chemicals mean that the farmers' fruit and vegetables can no longer be classified organic and therefore the farmers lose sales as foreign markets will no longer buy their produce. Although this is tackling malaria, it may be affecting farmers economically and hindering development in the area.
- The effects of malaria cost the African continent $12 billion every year.

Access to education in Africa

It has long been acknowledged that educating a nation is the key to ending the poverty cycle. However, access to adequate primary education is an ongoing issue in many African countries.

Case study: Education in Uganda

Uganda is a country in Africa struggling to provide adequate education for its young people. In a country with high birth rates and little educational infrastructure, it is hard to provide enough school places, despite attempts to introduce universal secondary education. Cash-flow problems with teachers' salaries and a lack of basic administration have meant that many teachers in the country have two or three jobs and can often struggle to attend school to teach children. This can lead to up to 40 per cent of teachers being absent long term and schools are facing dilemmas such as a lack of electricity and running water. Although school fees are paid for by the state, parents still have to pay for food, uniforms and textbooks, which few families can afford. Universal secondary school provision is the aim, although as yet it has not succeeded. Only 15 per cent of students in Uganda are female and although more people have access to education in the country now than previously, it is of a very poor standard.

According to UNESCO, 42 per cent of children in sub-Saharan Africa drop out of primary school. In countries such as Chad and Uganda, the drop-out rates are as high as 72 per cent and 68 per cent respectively. Although universal primary education is a Millennium Development Goal (see page 111), which many would have liked to have seen achieved by 2015, it is expected that at the current development rate this will only be possible by 2130.

Cash crops and trade

Many African countries are reliant on a single product for export and at the mercy of buyers from around the world. In Ethiopia, the average coffee-bean farmer lives on less than $2 a day, which cannot sustain his family. Ethiopia is one of the world's main producers of coffee beans and the country is reliant on this one product for trade with other countries. Indeed, 69 per cent of Ethiopia's exports are coffee beans and this makes up over 6 per cent of the country's GDP. Poor harvests and unfair trade agreements can hamper the economic growth of a country like Ethiopia. Although fair-trade initiatives have been introduced, unfair trade still exists and coffee and cocoa farmers often get less than 1 per cent of the price of the goods they provide.

Conflict

Africa is a very diverse continent and has a long history of conflict between different religious groups and often between governments/ dictators and civilians in the form of **civil war**. When conflict breaks out, it affects every aspect of people's lives; children can no longer go to school as people flee their homes, hospitals are overrun with

Key word

Civil war: A war between different groups in the same country.

casualties that they cannot treat, armed conflict destroys the social services that are in place and people escape to other countries and face being refugees. A lack of basic amenities such as shelter, sanitation and food means that many millions of Africans struggle to survive, let alone develop. The cost of armed conflict to Africa in the last fifteen years alone has been over $300 billion.

Figure 11.2 A child soldier involved in conflict in Africa

Case study: Conflict in South Sudan

As a relatively new country that sought its independence from Sudan in 2011 after civil war and peace talks, South Sudan faces many challenges and uncertainty. Conflict broke out in the country in December 2013 when tensions between President Salva Kiir and his deputy Riek Machar worsened and led to civil war after an attempted coup. The situation in 2014 was very serious; Oxfam stated that 3.7 million people needed immediate humanitarian aid, 7 million people were suffering from a lack of food security and 310,000 people had fled to neighbouring countries. Although there have been talks of a possible ceasefire, this is a long way from occurring and a lack of political, social and economic stability is a long-term problem for many people.

Case study: Boko Haram in Nigeria

Militant Islamist group Boko Haram has been responsible for the kidnapping of some 300 girls from schools in Nigeria, attacking officials and carrying out bombings. Nigeria is under civil unrest because of clashes between Christians and Muslims. Boko Haram members are of the belief that the way Nigeria is run is wrong and that they must do something to stop it. Their actions have caused international outrage and many high-profile campaigns have been run to see the kidnapped girls brought to safety (#BringBackOurGirls). The girls were kidnapped because it is Boko Haram's belief that girls should not be educated, and it disagrees with all such 'Westernised' ideas. The knock-on impact of this conflict is that many girls are no longer able to attend school for their own safety and many schools have had to shut down. Ten million young Nigerians are no longer in school and this has a huge effect on social and economic opportunities and the development of Nigeria.

Bad government and corruption

Developed countries are fortunate enough to have relatively stable governments that provide their people with the access to healthcare and education and the welfare they need. In the aftermath of colonialism and European leadership, a struggle for power and instability has emerged in many African countries. Many of these developing countries are not democratic and they face tyrannical leaders, a lack of human rights and no form of social or economic help. In the worst cases, dictators dramatically hinder development and conflict erupts from attempts to overthrow the oppressive government. Violence can break out after elections when people are forced to vote a certain way, and elections are often rigged. Members of opposition parties face violence or even death, along with their followers. In the 1990s, it was estimated that $200 billion was taken from the African people by bad governments, crippling social and economic progress.

Case study: Bad government and corruption in Nigeria

Nigeria is ranked 173rd out of 215 for countries that are fair and lacking corruption. It is ruled by an elite group of politicians who earn double the salary of an MP in Britain, and these policy-makers live in luxury with multiple homes around the globe. This is in stark contrast to the vast majority of the population who live on less than $2 a day. This makes Nigeria one of the most unequal countries in the world. Corruption is a huge factor that affects development and although the country has an estimated 40 billion barrels of crude oil and natural resources, the money for these commodities never reaches the average Nigerian – instead, the money goes to elite groups who steal power from the people (**kleptocracy**).

Despite having received over $385 million in aid over the last few decades, the country's economy is not growing and poverty for many is the worst it has ever been. The money given to the country has mostly gone to the elite and not to the people in the most desperate need.

Key word

Kleptocracy: A government in which those in power exploit the wealth of the country for their own personal gain.

Indeed, many international organisations have stated that bad government hinders development in the African continent more than any other factor, as it is the root cause of other problems like a lack of education and healthcare facilities. With armed conflict in no fewer than four countries, seventeen countries classified as authoritarian regimes, and only ten countries considered to have democratic institutions, it is no wonder that Africa is a continent of conflict.

Attempts to resolve a lack of development in Africa

Many developed countries around the world see it as their moral responsibility to help the African continent recover from its problems and develop. However, the enormous scale of Africa's social, economic and political issues means that providing countries with aid is very difficult to manage, organise and deliver to the people who are most in need. There are many ethical, economic and cultural implications of providing aid assistance, which can be given in many different guises, such as bilateral or multilateral aid or through non-government organisations (NGOs).

We will look at possible aid solutions to resolve Africa's multitude of problems and analyse their effectiveness.

Bilateral aid

Bilateral aid is given from a donor country to a recipient country. Every year the UK gives aid assistance to African countries through the Department for International Development (DFID). In 2014, two of the top five recipient countries of UK bilateral aid were in Africa – Ethiopia and Tanzania – which together received over £530 million. Many other major world powers, such as the USA, give bilateral aid to Africa. In 2013, the UK spent 0.7 per cent of its GDP on international aid (a target it had promised to hit for over a decade, but only committed to then). In a time of recession in Britain, however, many people are unhappy about £530 million being spent on international aid; this figure works out at £137 per British person and many feel that Britons should be spending the money on welfare in their own country in a time of austerity cuts. However, the government has advocated that it is an international obligation to help developing countries around the world that do not have the same social services and facilities enjoyed in Britain, and most people feel that citizens in other countries are worse off than themselves.

Case study: DFID and bilateral aid to Ethiopia in 2014

In 2014–15, the UK provided £356 million in aid to Ethiopia. Ethiopia experiences many serious economic, social and political problems, and 25 million people live in poverty. However, it has the fastest growing economy in Africa, is a large producer of agricultural products consumed by the West and is rich in natural resources. The DFID is involved in 30 development projects in the country that focus on developing better healthcare, increasing educational opportunities and improving food security. By 2015, the DFID should have:

- ensured another 2 million children have places in school
- given another 1.4 million people access to safer drinking water
- protected 1 million children from becoming infected with malaria through medical programmes.

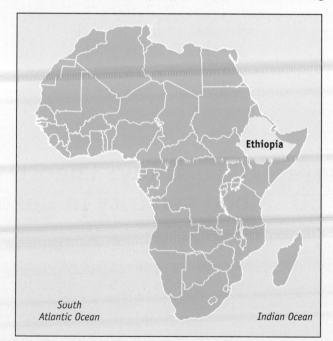

Figure 11.3 The location of Ethiopia

The effectiveness of bilateral aid

Bilateral aid is well funded and uses the resources available to whole governments. This means that the aid provided is based on a vast array of experience, experts and supplies. This type of aid in the UK is no longer tied aid, meaning its primary focus is those who are most in need rather than benefiting donor countries. However, there have been criticisms of bilateral aid provided by the DFID in recent years; a report in 2011 found that as many as 25 per cent of all projects failed to achieve their aims, and this has resulted in a review of cost-effectiveness within the Department. Failed projects include an educational pilot scheme in Kenya that had been running since 2005; over £55 million was spent on textbooks and classroom resources, many of which were stolen by corrupt gangs and sold on the black market. There was even evidence of people in Kenya making fraudulent claims for resources they never ordered, then claiming money from the DFID anyway. A separate report by *The Guardian* noted that millions of pounds of aid given to African countries has gone towards shopping centres and gated communities rather than to those most in need. Fraud, corruption and selling medicines and resources on the black market are challenges that all organisations providing aid to some parts of Africa face, and ensuring money and resources go to the people who need them is always a huge task.

Multilateral aid

Multilateral aid is given from a group of countries to a recipient country. This can be through international aid agreements or international organisations such as the African Union (AU), the European Union (EU) and the United Nations (UN).

Multilateral aid and the EU

The EU gives aid to African countries through EuropeAid. The EU's current aid budget is 0.44 per cent of its gross national income (GNI); a figure of $72 billion annually. The EU is the largest official donor of development assistance in the world and its main aims are to aid developing countries financially, support them in building their own infrastructure and promote human rights. EuropeAid has given over €850 million in aid to African countries since 1991.

Case study: Sierra Leone and the EU

In Sierra Leone, up to 70 per cent of the country's economy is dependent on agriculture. Yet in this country farming is carried out largely by hand, with few machines, tools or access to fertilisers. As a result of this, the EU set up an €11 million aid project to improve agricultural output, supporting up to 15,000 farmers. The result of the project was dramatically increased food security, more efficient farming methods, which were less labour intensive, and better marketing of produce.

Case study: The EU ensuring food security in Lesotho

A lack of agricultural yield and reliance on aid has reduced Lesotho's economic capacity. On top of this, the high HIV/AIDS prevalence has weakened farmers' immunities and abilities to work the land. The HIV/AIDS epidemic has affected the working-age population the most in Lesotho, reducing the food security of nearly half a million people. The EU spent nearly €700,000 on ensuring food security in Lesotho and the outcomes were:

- around 1360 households received education on how to improve crop production, with the help of expert volunteers
- around 1700 farmers received vouchers for buying seeds; this increased the diversity of crops being grown in the country, with families growing a few different products instead of just one – there are now different products for farmers to sell and nutrition has been improved through the added variety to people's diets.

Multilateral aid and the United Nations

The UN gives aid to African countries through its **specialised agencies**. There are many specialised agencies, but the ones that are best known for their work in Africa are:

- FAO (Food and Agriculture Organization)
- WHO (World Health Organization)
- UNICEF (United Nations International Children's Emergency Fund).

Millennium Development Goals (MDGs)

In 2000, the UN held a Millennium Summit that set eight development goals it wished to be achieved by 2015. These included to:

- eradicate extreme poverty and hunger
- achieve universal primary education for all
- promote gender equality
- reduce child mortality
- improve maternal health
- combat HIV/AIDS and malaria
- improve the environment
- create a global partnership to promote development.

It is intended that these goals be achieved by the end of 2015, and although major progress has been made with the help of UN aid, the problems that Africa faces are often too widespread to tackle completely. Each goal has had differing degrees of success.

> **Key word**
>
> **Specialised agency:** The UN is split into different organisations called 'specialised agencies'. Each specialised agency has a different remit and different goals for development, for example UNESCO (United Nations Educational, Scientific and Cultural Organization) may be concerned with providing fairer education for girls.

Case study: Food and Agriculture Organization in Somalia

The main aims of this agency are to reduce hunger, improve farming techniques and ensure food security for all. The agency works in almost every country in Africa to meet these aims, but some of its most recent projects have been in Somalia. Somalia is currently facing its worst famine for twenty years and an estimated 4 million people are affected. The rocketing price of food, war and failed crops have all contributed to the famine, which is affecting much of the Horn of Africa.

As a result of the FAO's work to provide humanitarian relief in the country, it has:

- given 158,333 farmers fertiliser and seeds
- set up a cash-for-work farming scheme that ensures income for local farmers
- improved the country's infrastructure by repairing some of the canals and roads.

It is also planning to immunise 14 million livestock and teach farmers how to look after them.

Case study: World Health Organization in Africa

The WHO works in 46 countries in Africa to improve the health of the African people. Its main aims are to reduce the prevalence of HIV/AIDS, malaria and polio and to provide immunisation programmes; one of its main programmes is the treatment and prevention of HIV/AIDS. In 2014–15, the WHO aimed to:

- provide antiretroviral treatment (ART) to 15 million people by 2015
- reduce the sexual transmission of HIV by 50 per cent
- prevent new HIV infections in children.

Previous programmes have seen new HIV infections reduced by 20 per cent since 2006.

Case study: United Nations International Children's Emergency Fund in Malawi

UNICEF's main aims are to improve children's rights, provide vaccination programmes for children and provide maternal health services. One such successful project has been the 1000 Special Days project, which has aimed to reduce malnutrition in Malawi. In that country, 50 per cent of under 5s suffer the effects of malnutrition, which include stunted growth and poor physical and mental development.

The project has aimed to:

- train local people in nutritional health
- provide nutrition to 200,000 mothers and 60,000 children
- look at tactics to improve diet diversity.

The effectiveness of multilateral aid

By far the largest benefit of multilateral aid, compared to other types of aid, is how well funded it is: the combined funding of several groups of countries means that larger, more effective projects can be undertaken that are likely to reach more people and be better resourced. This type of aid is also argued to be more reliable than other types: donor countries feel safer donating to a project involving several countries, where the economic burden can be shared. However, the work of multilateral organisations can be minimal in countries that are not democracies as giving to these countries does not ensure that resources or money go to the people in most need. Also, bad government, violence and civil war within some African countries all limit what agencies can do.

Non-government organisations (NGOs)

NGOs provide aid to developing countries through charitable donations. Some of the most famous NGOs include Save the Children, Oxfam, Christian Aid, WaterAid and the Red Cross. These organisations work on a variety of different levels, often on regional or local projects within different countries, and on a smaller scale than multilateral aid. Relying on charitable funding reduces the funds available to NGOs, but the advantage is that they can set their own aid agendas and are not influenced by governments.

Case study: Oxfam in Niger

Niger is one of the poorest countries in Africa. It is ranked 186 out of 186 of the least-developed countries in the world (according to the Human Development Index). Life expectancy is 54 years, nearly 3 million people lack food security and 70 per cent of the country's 16 million people live on less than $1 a day. These problems have been exacerbated by poor harvests, famine and rising food prices.

Oxfam is aiming to help around 680,000 people in Niger by providing food aid and assistance with farming and livestock. It has also provided thousands of food vouchers to starving people to allow them to buy food instead of begging. This has had a hugely positive impact in the area by providing very effective emergency relief aid. However, there are limits to this work; it may help people who are already in crisis, but NGO aid often has a limited long-term effect and does little to solve the factors that hinder development.

Figure 11.4 Oxfam logo

Case study: Save the Children in Tanzania

Save the Children is an NGO that works in many countries across the African continent, reaching thousands of people a day. It has run several successful aid programmes in Tanzania, such as the Kangaroo Care Programme. This programme aimed to save the lives of newborn babies who are often underweight or premature. Save the Children found that nearly one-third of children under five who die lose their lives before they are a month old and, as a result of this, it set up centres in 21 hospitals in the region to teach mothers how to look after their babies. It is reckoned that this programme saved the lives of 3000 babies in 2011 alone, and many mothers were also given support and help to look after themselves post-birth to improve maternal health. Again, these types of projects offer invaluable support and help to many thousands of people every year, providing emergency food aid and longer-term health and education projects. They still have their limitations though; Save the Children is often restricted in what it can do in war zones and it is reliant on charitable donations. It also works on a smaller scale than many multilateral and bilateral aid projects.

Effectiveness of NGOs

NGOs undeniably provide essential life-saving humanitarian aid to many thousands of people in African countries. Their work impacts on communities by improving access to education and safe drinking water, and is vital during times of international emergency. However, many people have criticised the work of NGOs, as a lot of money donated to them is spent on bureaucracy and administration rather than directly on the people in need. Also, they usually work on a smaller scale than multilateral and bilateral approaches and many small NGOs can be working on the same issues in the same areas rather than taking on larger and more successful projects.

Chapter 12

International issues: Questions and model answers

Question and model answer

Question ?

To what extent does the political system of a world power you have studied effectively scrutinise the government? **20 marks**

Responses will be credited that make reference to:

- a description and analysis of the ways the US political system checks the government
- a balanced overall evaluative comment on the effectiveness of the US political system in scrutinising the government
- a clear, coherent line of argument.

Up to **8 marks** for knowledge (description, explanation and exemplification) and up to **12 marks** for analysis and structured answers.

Remember

Knowledge questions will have either 12 or 20 marks allocated and you will answer one question from a choice of two. If an answer contains more analytical/evaluative points than are required to gain the allocation of 4 marks, these can be credited as knowledge and understanding marks.

Model answer

The Federal System of Government in the USA is made up of three branches: the President (Executive), the Congress (Legislative) and the Supreme Court (Judicial). The President is often viewed as the most important person in the USA political system, but the system is based upon the Constitution which ensures that each of the three branches has different, separate powers which prevents the President from becoming too powerful. The Congress and the Supreme Court provide checks on the powers of the President. The US system of government has been described as 'Compromise, compromise, compromise'.

The President of the USA has many important legislative powers such as proposing new laws to Congress. At the State of the Union Address, the President often outlines new policy ideas such as the Affordable Care Act (Obamacare) or Tax Reforms. This allows the President to put forward his party's ideology and express what he would like Congress to achieve over the next few years giving him great power. However, this power can

be severely limited by Congress who have to vote on Presidential proposals. After the Mid Term elections in 2010, the Republicans now dominate the House of Representatives meaning that it is harder for Barack Obama to pass policies. Therefore, the Congress can effectively scrutinise the President's actions, and provide effective checks on the political system, to a large extent.

Whilst in power, Barack Obama also has the power to veto any laws which Congress passes; if he does not agree with them, he does not have to sign them. This means that the law is not passed and that it can go back to the Congress again for reconsideration. During his time in Office Obama has used his veto twice, blocking legislation such as the Interstate Recognition of Notarizations Act. However, this can be overturned by the Congress with a two-thirds majority vote, meaning that the President can never block laws which the majority of representatives believe is in the interest of the country. This provides an effective check on the political system to a large extent.

The President also has the power to appoint Justices of the Supreme Court. For example, Obama appointed Sonia Sotomayor to the Supreme Court, making her the first Hispanic person to hold the position. This means that if vacancies occur the President can appoint judges sympathetic to the political views of the President. However, the Senate must approve all appointments to the Supreme Court and once appointed, the Justices cannot be removed by the President. The Supreme Court also provides effective checks on the political system as it can deem any of the President's proposals 'unconstitutional'. This means that the Supreme Court can force the Congress and President to reconsider aspects of any law proposals which violate the Constitution. In July 2014 the Supreme Court declared that the President had acted unconstitutionally when he appointed people to the boards of a federal agency while the Senate was technically still in session. So the legislature and judiciary can effectively scrutinise the actions of the government.

Lastly, the President is the Commander-in-Chief of the Armed Forces making him an extremely powerful man. This means that he can send troops overseas for up to 60 days without the backing of the Congress. However, he cannot declare war – only Congress can do this – and this prevents one branch of the government from having too much power and ensures America is democratic.

Overall, the political system of the USA is split into separate branches which ensures that great scrutiny can be made on the powers of the president. The system of checks and balances ensures that decisions in America must be agreed by most representatives to ensure democracy and limit the President's powers to a large extent. However many argue that the hostility of the dominant Republican House of Representatives towards Obama is leading to gridlock in government and that this creates a weak Presidency and weak government.

Marker's comment

This is an excellent answer as it covers a range of relevant points. The structure of the answer clarifies the issue with clear and consistent lines of argument. A range of developed points with accurate analytical comments are made that are justified and exemplified. This answer also provides balance by offering counter-arguments that are relevant and insightful. The conclusion is balanced and insightful and directly addresses the central part of the question, going beyond the question to hint that the checks and balance system threatens good government. This answer would gain full marks. **20/20**

Question and model answer

Remember

Knowledge questions will have either 12 or 20 marks allocated and you will answer one question from a choice of two. If an answer contains more analytical/evaluative points than are required to gain the allocation of 4 marks, these can be credited as knowledge and understanding marks.

Question ?

A world power has influence and power in international relations.

Discuss with reference to a world power you have studied. **20 marks**

Responses will be credited that make reference to:

- the role and analysis of the influence and power of China in international relations
- balance overall evaluative comment of the influence and power of China in international relations
- a clear, coherent line of argument.

Up to **8 marks** for knowledge (description, explanation and exemplification) and up to **12 marks** for analysis and structured answers.

115

Model answer

China is a very important country in terms of influence and power; it has the largest population in the world (1.3 billion people) and has the second largest economy (after the USA). It is often thought to be an 'emerging super-power' with an important role in International Organisations such as the G20 and the United Nations (UN). China's role in the international community is increasing socially, economically and politically; something which will be discussed here.

Economically, China has the second largest economy in the world after the USA, and it is the world's largest exporter of goods. It may only have 7% of the world's farmland, but it produces 21% of the world's food as well as being nicknamed the 'factory of the world'. China's annual economic growth has never been less than 7% in the last three decades, meaning it is an economically powerful country, especially during the economic recession. However as China becomes wealthier, and it develops further in service industries, its reputation as a producer of cheap goods is decreasing in favour of cheaper labour elsewhere in the developing world.

Given its economic strength, China is now a major player in the G20 group and in global financial relations. For example, in 2013 Xi Jinping attended his first G20 Summit in Russia where he played a key role in talks to ensure global economic security. China is currently responsible for around 30% of global economic growth, and along with the USA, it has taken steps towards stabilising international debt, showing its key economic influence in international relations.

Clear evidence of China's new confidence and growing military power is reflected in her growing presence in south-east Asia and her challenge to American dominance. China is in dispute with Vietnam over territorial claims and is the only country with some influence in North Korea. The independence of Taiwan creates friction with the USA and it is clear that China now sees herself as the superpower of the Asian countries – clear evidence of her growing international status.

Politically, China is a member of other International Organisations such as the United Nations (UN). China has played an active role in the UNEP (United Nations Environmental Programme) and has pledged to spend nearly $468 million in making its economy greener. It has also played key roles in international decision making, as China has one of the five permanent seats on the UN Security Council. This means that China can hold the balance of power in important decisions about peacekeeping missions and UN sanctions against aggressors. For example in 2012 China, along with Russia, vetoed planned action in Syria to condemn the Assad regime and provide emergency assistance in the country. This caused friction between East and West with China and Russia preventing action from being taken which the UK, USA and France wanted to go ahead. Therefore, China can hold the balance of political power in important international issues, demonstrating how politically powerful the country has become in international relations.

Marker's comment

The structure of the answer clarifies the issue with clear and consistent lines of argument. A range of developed points with accurate analytical comments are made that are justified and exemplified. This answer also provides balance by offering counter-arguments that are relevant and insightful. The conclusion is balanced and insightful and directly addresses the central part of the question. This answer would gain full marks. **20/20**

Question and model answer

Question ?

To what extent has a world issue you have studied been resolved by international organisations? **20 marks**

Responses will be credited that make reference to:

- the responses of international organisations to development issues in Africa
- analysis of the ways international organisations attempt to resolve development issues in Africa
- balanced overall evaluative comment on the extent to which responses made by international organisations have been successful in resolving development issues in Africa
- a clear, coherent line of argument.

Up to **8 marks** for knowledge (description, explanation and exemplification) and up to **12 marks** for analysis and structured answers.

Remember

Knowledge questions will have either 12 or 20 marks allocated and you will answer one question from a choice of two. If an answer contains more analytical/evaluative points than are required to gain the allocation of 4 marks, these can be credited as knowledge and understanding marks.

Model answer

Development on the African continent is a very important world issue. Lack of development in African countries is a long standing issue caused by social, economic and political problems. However, many international organisations such as the UN have tried to resolve issues in African countries through aid projects and UN peacekeepers which have had varying levels of success.

The UN has aimed to have universal primary education in Africa by 2015 as part of the Millennium Development Goals. One UN agency in particular, UNICEF, has been involved in improving this. Lack of education is a massive factor that hinders development in Africa, as education is often the best way to lift children out of poverty and improve their futures. In 2014, UNICEF continued to roll out its 'Schools for Africa' campaign, which aimed to raise a further $80 million to put towards education in thirteen African countries. This has been successful to a large extent as primary school enrolment has risen in these thirteen countries and there have been successful life skills programmes rolled out to raise awareness of HIV/AIDS. This has given more children a chance to improve their job opportunities in the future and help them try

to escape poverty. However, despite all the work carried out by UNICEF, there is still a lot of countries such as Somalia which have very poor education systems. In Somalia the enrolment rate is only 23%. UNICEF has had a fair amount of success in helping Africa develop in terms of education but there is still a massive amount of progress to be made.

The WFP is another UN agency that has aimed to resolve lack of development in Africa by tackling hunger. Hunger is a massive problem in Africa due to high rates of poverty and lack of effective farming methods. The WFP launched their 'Food Voucher Programme' in 2012 in Somalia, which went on to help over 15,000 people. This gave families up to $80 of vouchers a month to buy food from local markets which in turn reduced hunger and boosted the local economy. Despite this success on a small scale, the hunger problem in Africa is still too big for international organisations to overcome, with over 30 million starving people in Africa. Political and social problems in African countries also hinder attempts at resolving poverty and hunger. In Somalia in 2011, the WFP also sent large food donations which ⇒

117

⇒

were stolen and sold on the black market. This shows that WFP have not had great success in promoting development, as hunger is such a massive obstacle to overcome and often conflict within African countries can hinder effective aid from being delivered.

At present a civil war is raging in the new state of South Sudan. In 2013 the President Salva Kiir sacked the vice-president Riek Machar and ethnic conflict and armed conflict broke out. Prior to its independence in 2011 abundant international aid and access to oil revenue suggested that South Sudan would be a prosperous country. However the leaders of the new government used much of this money to expand the army and to enrich themselves. So the financial support of international organisations has not been used to benefit the people and this highlights the limitation of international organisation's support.

The UN has sent 10 000 peacekeepers to South Sudan and the international community is trying to broker a peace deal to end the civil war. The UN Security Council is considering an arms ban on the warring factions. More than one million of South Sudan's six million have fled their homes and the country is on the brink of famine. The UN supported by the EU has set up five refugee camps. So international organisations have been effective in feeding and protecting refugees but it has not been effective in preventing the civil war. However the blame lies with the new ruling elite of South Sudan.

To conclude, international organisations such as the UN and the EU have made some major progress in promoting development in African countries on a small scale, but they have faced problems overall development because of the vast problems the continent faces like hunger and lack of education. The situation in South Sudan highlights the difficulties facing international organisation, despite massive international aid the country is in ruin.

Marker's comment

This is an excellent answer as it covers a range of points. The structure of the answer clarifies the issue with clear and consistent lines of argument. A range of developed points with accurate analytical comments are made that are justified and exemplified. It provides excellent up-to-date exemplification. This answer also provides balance by offering counter-arguments that are relevant and insightful. The conclusion is balanced and insightful and directly addresses the central part of the question. This answer would gain full marks.   **20/20**

Part Five: Source-based questions

Chapter 13
Selectivity and conclusions questions

There are two types of skills questions that you will have practised in class. These are:

1 using sources of information to identify **to what extent is it accurate to state that ...**

2 using sources of information to identify **what conclusions can be drawn**.

These questions will be allocated 8 marks and will appear in any two of the three sections of the course exam. There will be no choice of source-based questions, for example in the exam paper if there is a Social Issues source-based question it will be either on Social Inequality or Crime and the Law; if there is an International Issues source-based question it will be either on World Powers or World Issues.

Remember

'To what extent is it accurate to state that ...' question

In the question that follows, you are required to evaluate two complex sources, detecting and explaining selectivity. You must show evidence that supports the extent of accuracy of the given viewpoint.

For full marks, evidence from both sources must be cited that both supports and opposes the given view.

For full marks, you **must** make an overall judgement as to the extent of the accuracy of the given view. You can only be awarded a maximum of 6 marks if you make no overall judgement on the extent of the accuracy of the statement.

Remember that up to 2 marks are also available for accurate comment/analysis of the origin and reliability of the sources.

Remember

In your course exam the source-based questions will appear in any two of the three units.

These questions will have at least two sources and be allocated 8 marks.

You can gain a maximum of 3 marks for a single developed point, depending on your use of the evidence and the quality of your analysis/evaluation.

For full marks you must refer to all the sources in your answer.

Question ?

Study Sources A and B below then attempt the question that follows.

Source A

The 2010 General Election televised debates

The 2010 General Election witnessed the first live television debates between leaders from each of the three main UK parties – Conservatives, Labour and the Liberal Democrats. Cameron, Brown and Clegg all hoped to visually connect with voters during a tightly fought campaign nicknamed the 'digital election'.

Before the first-ever debate of its kind, an Ipsos MORI poll revealed 60% of those voters surveyed felt the TV debates would be important to them in helping decide the way they would vote. The performance of the candidates during the debates could also have the potential to alter the way the media would handle coverage of each of the leaders and their parties. Following the debates, a range of polls suggested Nick Clegg had won convincingly, with many voters indicating they would switch to the Liberal Democrats. The success of Nick Clegg led to claims of 'Cleggmania' and a prediction of a historic increase in the number of seats for the Liberal Democrats.

A second survey conducted after the election by an independent polling organisation found the leaders' TV debates changed the voting intentions of more than a million voters. Put another way, the results indicated that the debates altered the voting behaviour of more than 4% of the electorate. Also, it could be argued that TV coverage of the leaders' debate motivated thousands of voters to use their vote when otherwise they may not have done. In some parts of the country there was a rise of 17% in younger voters indicating that they would turn out to vote. On the other hand, it could be argued that the TV debates only reinforced the existing views most people had.

A third survey from the British Election Study 2010 found 9.4m people watched the first live debate on ITV, 4.5m watched the second debate on Sky and 8.5m the final debate on the BBC. After the second debate, polling figures suggested Cameron and Clegg were joint winners. After the third debate, polling figures suggested Cameron was the winner. Overall, the results from this study appeared to suggest 12% of voters changed their mind about which party to vote for as a consequence of watching the TV election debates.

After the polling stations closed and the votes were counted, it was found that no one party had an overall majority in the House of Commons. The Conservatives obtained the largest share of the overall vote polling 36% (up 3.7% from 2005), Labour attracted 29% of the vote (down 6.2% from 2005) and the Liberal Democrats 23% (up 1% from 2005).

(Adapted from various sources)